ARBITRATION LAW AND PROCEDURE

 ⁊ **LIBRARY SERVICE**

ɔefore the last date shown
ᴇsted by other borrowers)
application

OF /00/46

MICHAEL FORDE

Arbitration Law and Procedure

WITH A FOREWORD BY

The Honourable Mr Justice Dermot Kinlen
of the High Court

THE ROUND HALL PRESS

The book was typeset by
Gilbert Gough Typesetting for
THE ROUND HALL PRESS
Kill Lane, Blackrock, Co. Dublin.
and in the United States of America by
THE ROUND HALL PRESS
c/o International Specialized Book Services,
5804 NE Hassalo Street, Portland, OR 97213

A catalogue record for this book
is available from the British Library

ISBN 1-85800-032-7

**Printed in Ireland by
Betaprint, Dublin**

For Edward

FOREWORD

Arbitration is a popular alternative for the resolution of disputes. It can be less complex, more expeditious and cheaper than the cost of going to Court. In many disputes the arbitrator has material skills to help the parties to a final conclusion which are not normally found in Judges. However, the clearness and efficiency of an arbitration procedure depends greatly on the individual arbitrator. Indeed the pre-arbitration meeting when normally the arbitrator lays down the time scale for taking various steps such as discovery and interchange of documents or pleadings clarifying the issues is often the crucial element in the expedition and conclusion of an arbitration. Normally there is no appeal from the decision of the arbitrator. The Courts are and should be slow to intervene in the arbitration. The parties have freely chosen arbitration as the method for resolving their dispute. The fact is very few arbitrations are ever considered in the Law Courts. Most of the so-called 'leading cases' belong to an ethos and time long past. The Courts, indeed, could learn with advantage the proper streamlining of arbitration proceedings in order to expedite more cases and reduce costs.

In my student days there were very few Irish sources available. We were mainly dependent on English textbooks but with the passage of time they had become greatly irrelevant and in fact were capable of misleading a student. The restructuring of the law of property in 1925 in England, for example, had left many textbooks nearly useless in this jurisdiction. In those days we relied on Kiely's excellent book on equity when we were lucky enough to have access to a copy. Mr Sandes, quietly working away in the Law Library, produced three editions of his outline of criminal law. However, the main sources of legal inspiration were in the late Brendan McCormack's notes and the still invaluable notes of Kevin Waldron, now Director of Education at the King's Inns, Dublin.

Nowadays the picture has changed utterly. There are a wide variety of excellent textbooks and learned articles available for the serious student, practising lawyer, legal researcher and enthusiastic members of the judiciary. All the writers are to be encouraged for their industry, clarity of expression and erudition. Certainly the financial rewards in producing an

Irish textbook are very small. Dr Michael Forde has been a prolific producer of Irish legal textbooks. Most of them are of use throughout the common law world including his present volume on Arbitration Law and Procedure. He deserves the gratitude of all practitioners in the field of arbitration. His book is directed not merely to lawyers but to all persons involved in this extremely significant and growing area. Arbitration is not merely a local matter governed only by local Acts but is of international importance. I sincerely hope that Dr Michael Forde, who in such a short period has been so productive, will continue to help not only the Irish legal system but his worldwide readers by his clear and concise exposition of so many branches of law. This book is essential for all people involved in arbitration.

Dermot Kinlen,
The High Court, Dublin.

14 June 1994

PREFACE

The law of arbitration is concerned with procedures for deciding disputes outside the ordinary court system. Usually the arbitrator is not a qualified lawyer but he will have some knowledge of the law and may take legal advice when appropriate. There are certain types of arbitration which are mainly conducted by lawyers. In some countries judges are permitted to conduct the occasional arbitration but that is not the practice in Ireland, due to a questionable view taken about the constitutional position of the judiciary.

In this book I have sought to set out the legal rules regarding domestic arbitration in Ireland. For the time being these rules also apply to international arbitrations subject to Irish law. But is seems that the UNCITRAL model law may be enacted in the not too distant future to govern non-indigenous arbitrations. In a great number of respects Irish arbitration law is identical to the law in England, especially before the 1979 reforms there. Accordingly any author of a work on this topic is very indebted to Mustill & Boyd's classic, *Commercial Arbitration* (2nd edition, 1989), which is the definitive book on the topic. Dealing with those areas where Irish and English law are the same, I tend to set out the position in a summary fashion here and the reader should consult Mustill & Boyd for a more detailed exposition of the English authorities. Another book which I have found extremely useful is Bernstein's *Handbook of Arbitration Practice* (2nd edition, 1993), which contains very useful practical advice and suggestions for the day to day conduct of arbitrations, as well as descriptions of some of the more specialised types of arbitration.

The law as stated here is on the basis of material available to me on 1 May 1994. A problem always in setting out the Irish law on a subject is the 'unreported judgment'—a written decision which has not got into the law reports. There seems to be quite a number of these on arbitration issues and I have done my best to refer to them. However, many of these deal almost exclusively with facts and there is practically no sustained legal reasoning, which perhaps explains why they were not reported. No doubt some of these elusive judicial masterpieces have escaped my attention.

Once again Maria Armah-Kwantreng typed the manuscript with formidable speed and accuracy. Michael Adams of The Round Hall Press has been a most supportive editor and Terri McDonnell, also of The Round Hall Press, has again been extremely diligent in marketing the book. The 'usual suspects', Catherine, Peter and Patrick, have provided good-humoured encouragement throughout this endeavour, for which I am profoundly grateful. Finally, a special work of thanks to Mr Justice Kinlen for his foreword to the book; he was most generous to me when he practised at the Bar and his qualities of compassion and his sound judgment of individuals and circumstances are presently being outstandingly displayed on the Bench.

M.F.
Mountain View Road
Dublin.

Bloomsday 1994

CONTENTS

TABLE OF STATUTES

TABLE OF CASES

INTRODUCTORY

Arbitration is a common form of dispute-resolution procedure which is often resorted to in place of litigation.[1] There is considerable variety in the manner in which particular arbitrations are conducted, ranging from highly informal procedures to an approach resembling the conduct of High Court actions. All depends on the nature of the dispute and the type of arbitral tribunal the parties have selected. However, all arbitrations have certain essential characteristics, which have been summed up as follows:

(a) there is a dispute or difference between the parties which has been formulated in some way or other;

(b) the dispute or difference has been remitted by the parties to the person to resolve in such manner that he is called upon to exercise a judicial function;

(c) where appropriate, the parties must have been provided with an opportunity to present evidence and/or submissions in support of their respective claims in the dispute;

(d) the parties have agreed to accept his decision.[2]

METHODS OF DISPUTE-RESOLUTION

There are many types of dispute that can arise between persons and several methods exist through which disputes can be resolved, including arbitration.

Negotiation Negotiation between the disputing parties or their representatives is undoubtedly the best technique. It is more economical than many of the other modes and, if a settlement is reached, there will be neither

1   The definitive text is M. Mustill & S. Boyd, *Commercial Arbitration* (2nd ed. 1989), which will be referred to throughout as *Mustill & Boyd*. See also A. Walton & M. Vitoria, ed., *Russell on Arbitration* (20th ed. 1982).
2   *Arenson v. Arenson* [1977] AC 405, at p. 428.

winners nor losers; settlement suggests that each side is reasonably content with the outcome. Especially where the parties in dispute intend to continue dealing with each other, they will far prefer negotiation to calling in lawyers and consequent confrontations, which could easily sour a mutually beneficial relationship.

Mediation   Where negotiations are proving especially difficult to conduct, it can help to have mediation. This involves a third-party intervening, bringing proposals and counter-proposals to the parties and encouraging them to settle the matter. A skilful mediator can help to resolve the apparently most intractable of problems.

Expertise   An arbitrator is often contrasted with an expert, frequently a valuer, who is called in to determine a matter that two or more parties cannot agree on. Experts are called upon, for instance, to value shares in companies when some of the members seek to buy-out others, or to ascertain what rent should be paid under a tenancy agreement which provides for third-party determination of the matter. As is explained below, strictly the expert does not resolve a dispute between parties; if he indeed is deciding a formulated dispute, then very likely he is acting as an arbitrator and not as an expert only.

Litigation   The route through which many persons travel in order to resolve their differences is litigation, that is, resort to the courts. Normally they will be represented by lawyers and, unless they settle in advance of the court hearing, their dispute will be aired in the public arena.[3] There are fairly rigid procedures laid down for the conduct of litigation—in the District Court, in the Circuit Court and in the High Court. Occasionally the nature of the dispute makes it appropriate to be dealt with in a court-like administrative tribunal, for instance the Employment Appeals Tribunal. There is also the Labour Court which exercises some judicial-type functions in the industrial relations field.

Arbitration   Finally there is arbitration—the appointment of one or more individuals to decide the dispute in a manner which is legally binding on the parties. This process is preferable to litigation and also to expertise in several respects, although those alternative processes may be preferable in particular circumstances. Even though arbitration does not connote dealing with lawyers and going to court, often lawyers will be involved in the matter

3   *Re R. Ltd* [1989] IR 126.

and it may be necessary to make certain applications to the High Court. Where the issue in dispute is overwhelmingly a technical one, it may be possible to dispense altogether with lawyers or at least greatly reduce their role in the entire affair. The following are the main advantages of arbitration over litigation.

i. *Confidentiality*—Unlike court cases, arbitrations are conducted behind closed doors. Parties therefore have the assurance that highly confidential information that may emerge in the course of a reference does not get into the public domain.

ii. *Choice of adjudicator*—In a court case the parties have no say whatsoever over which judge will hear their dispute; they must accept whoever is allocated to their case by the usual machinery for the assignment of judges. One of the parties may regret later that the judge he got did not fully understand the issues or the evidence, or was some way inexcusably unsympathetic to his case. In arbitration, by contrast, the disputing parties are free to select whoever they wish (and is available) to arbitrate between them. If the dispute is about the quality of commodities or about financial dealings, a person with a background in those fields probably will be preferred. If there are significant legal issues, they may select a lawyer competent in the area in question. They may even opt for two or more arbitrators, depending on the nature of their dispute. At times, before commencing on the reference, the chosen arbitrator may seek to mediate the dispute and, even during the reference, some efforts at mediation may be attempted.

iii. *Procedural flexibility*—Provided certain minimum standards of fair procedure are adhered to, the parties, or they and the arbitrator, can determine exactly what procedure should be followed in conducting the reference. There are many arbitrations for which specially designed procedural rules have been prescribed in advance; for instance, several trade associations have their own rules of procedure for arbitrations conducted under their aegis.[4] In Ireland the Chartered Instituted of Arbitrators have published a set of model rules which are quite popular;[5] the parties may agree that those rules should be followed, or those rules subject to certain modifications.

iv. *Location*—The reference will be conducted wherever the parties, or they and the arbitrator, decide on.

---

4   E.g. the 'GAFTA', that is, Grain and Feed Trade Association Rules.
5   Reproduced post pp. 149 et seq.

v. *Speed*—At times arbitration can be much quicker than litigation. On other occasions, especially if the arbitrator does not keep a tight control of the reference, it can be prolonged for a inordinate period.

vi. *Enforcement abroad*—Where it will be necessary to enforce the adjudication in another country, especially outside of the European Union, there are distinct advantages with arbitration. For most countries of the world are parties to an international convention which greatly facilitates the mutual enforcement of each other's arbitration awards.[6]

DEFINING ARBITRATION

While readers will have a general picture of what arbitration consists of, it is necessary to clarify exactly what is involved in the process. This is not just a matter of abstract academic interest; a clear definition will help in resolving many practical problems that can arise in the course of a reference. Additionally, there are disputes-resolution procedures that resemble arbitration, in particular, valuation by an expert. If, on closer inspection, what appears to be a valuation possesses the essential characteristics of an arbitration, then it is governed by the Arbitration Act, 1954 ('the 1954 Act') and the principles set out in this book.

There is no statutory definition for the arbitral process. The closest the 1954 Act comes to a definition is the meaning it gives to the term 'arbitration agreement' for the purpose of that Act—being a 'written agreement to refer present or future differences to arbitration, whether an arbitrator is named therein or not.'[7] Very few reported cases address squarely the issue of definition. In two leading modern cases[8] the question of definition is touched on and in one of them the 'indicia' of an arbitration are summarised.[9] But the issue being decided there was whether or to what extent do valuers enjoy the same immunity from liability in negligence as is conferred on arbitrators carrying on a reference.

In their definitive treatise on the subject, Mustill & Boyd[10] set out the essential characteristics of an arbitration as follows.

6   The New York Convention on the Recognition and Enforcement of Foreign Arbitral Awards, of 1958; in 1st schedule to the Arbitration Act, 1980.
7   S. 2(1).
8   *Sutcliffe v. Thackrah* [1974] AC 727 and *Arenson v. Arenson* [1977] AC 405.
9   Supra p. 1, n.2.
10   At pp. 38 et seq.

Decision intended to be binding   The essence of a submission to arbitration is that it is a contract to honour and carry out the arbitrator's decision; it authorises him to make a binding legal determination of the rights of the parties. Conversely, an agreement for non-binding arbitration, even if written, is not regarded at common law or under the 1954 Act as an arbitration agreement for the purposes of Arbitration Law.

Same parties to the agreement and the dispute   The written agreement must be between parties who are in dispute or whose future dispute is envisaged. If both parties to the dispute are not parties to the agreement, the matter is outside the 1954 Act.[11] An agreement that permits only one of the parties to refer the matter to arbitration can be within the Act. In England, a procedure whereby a dispute between employees and a trade union, regarding terms of employment, could be determined by an arbitration tribunal, at the behest of a Government Minister, was held not to be an arbitration for the purpose of the Arbitration Act.[12] This was because 'the arbitration must be between parties to [the arbitration] agreement; and it must be as to a mater which they have agreed to refer to arbitration.'[13] Although the union and the employer there were involved in an arbitration, they were never parties to an agreement to have that matter arbitrated. The agreement was one between the employer and the Government.

Consensual tribunal   The arbitrator's power to make decisions binding on the parties derives entirely from the agreement of those parties, rather than from some external source. Of course, the agreement does not have to nominate the arbitrator; it can leave that matter to be decided by the parties in due course. Frequently, arbitration agreements stipulate that the arbitrator shall be chosen by a designated person or body, such as the Chairman of the Bar Council, the President of the Incorporated Law Society, or the International Chamber of Commerce. Although in a sense the parties in such cases have not chosen the arbitrator, they nevertheless agreed to the procedure for selecting the arbitrator. Where a party does not appoint an arbitrator or a vacancy arises which cannot be filled, the 1954 Act gives the court authority by default to make an appointment.[14] Also the extent of the arbitrator's power in this regard cannot range any wider than that conferred on him by agreement.

11   *Pittalis v. Sherefettim* [1986] 2 All E.R. 227.
12   *Imperial Metal Industries (Kynoch) Ltd v. Amalg. Union of Engineering Workers* [1979] ICR 23.
13   Id. at p.34. See also *Baron v. Sunderland Corp.* [1966] 2 QB 60.
14   S. 18; see post p. 43-44.

However, arbitrators acting under special statutory provisions[15] are often not appointed by the parties or their chosen mechanism of appointment. And, under Part IV of the 1954 Act, the Circuit Court or the High Court can appoint an arbitrator to resolve certain issues that have arisen in litigation before the court.

A formulated dispute   The agreement must be one which contemplates the resolution of a formulated dispute and, when the reference commences, a formulated dispute must be in existence. So-called valuation agreements, that is, to determine the value of property or of services, may or may not be agreements to arbitrate; it is because of this uncertainty that the common 'as experts' clause often is inserted in such agreements. As was said in *Sutcliffe v. Thackrah*,[16] which concerned an architect appointed to value work done in the course of building a house,

> One of the features of an arbitration is that there is a dispute between two or more persons who agree that they will refer their dispute to the adjudication of some selected person whose decision upon the matter they agree to accept. As an example, the dispute may involve an issue as to what a particular article is worth or as the value of work that has been done. It follows that the task of an arbitrator may in some cases be the task of arriving at a valuation. In some circumstances, therefore, someone might be regarded both as a valuer and an arbitrator. But it by no means follows that everyone who has a duty of valuing, a duty which obviously must be fairly and honestly discharged, is an arbitrator.[17]

The test of whether a person selected to make a valuation is an arbitrator or simply a valuer, it would seem, is whether, under the contract, he is automatically part of a process for completing the substantive agreement. If the parties envisage a valuation being made and designate a person to do that job, he acts simply as a valuer. For instance, where the parties agree to purchase goods or shares at a price to be determined by X, they have not agreed to arbitration by X about the price. In *Carr v. Phelan*,[18] the parties had agreed on the purchase of a ground rent and designated the county registrar as arbitrator to fix the price. It was held that, notwithstanding his description, the county registrar was acting only as a valuer here. On the other hand, if, under the contract, a person is held in reserve and only becomes involved where the parties are in dispute about the proper valuation, he is an arbitrator.

15   Infra pp. 14 et seq.   16 [1974] AC 727.
17   Id. at p. 745.   18 [1976-7] ILRM 149.

Kingston v. Layden[19] is one of the few reported cases where the court had to decide whether the decision-making procedure was indeed arbitration. A dispute had arisen between the plaintiff and the defendant, who owned adjoining coal mines in Co. Roscommon, regarding alleged encroachments by them on each other's properties and taking out coal belonging to the other. Proceedings were commenced but the parties, by a written consent, agreed to stay the action and have many of the issues resolved by a surveyor with an expertise in mining. This agreement provided *inter alia* that the surveyor should hear the parties, that his report should be binding on them and accepted as conclusive, that the party in default should be obliged to pay the other's costs and expenses, and that the submission could be made a rule of court at the expense of either party. Following a lengthy investigation of occurrences over several years, the surveyor published a report which called on the defendant to pay a substantial sum as compensation and which set out the future boundaries between the parties' properties. The question then arose whether the report's findings were binding on the parties in litigation arising from the trespasses, which led to a consideration of whether the surveyor had acted as an arbitrator or as an appraiser. According to Johnston J, 'an appraisement, generally speaking, is the written finding of an appraiser or valuer, appointed by two parties on account of his expert knowledge of the subject-matter, or of some special aptitude that he possesses, to report as to some matter in respect of which no difference had yet arisen between the parties, such report (generally a valuation as to price, or an estimate as to value) being obtained for the purpose of preventing the arising of future differences or litigation between the parties, and being based upon the appraiser's own skill and knowledge, without hearing evidence or arguments.'[20] Apart from being chosen for his expertise, it was held that the surveyor's determination of the issues had none of these features and, accordingly, his report was an arbitration award.

Enforceable agreement to arbitrate Since the very essence of arbitration is an agreement to honour the award, one would have thought that, where a party declined to go to arbitration, he could be compelled to do so. But that is not strictly the law; in the past one party could relatively easily and with impunity frustrate the conduct of the reference. It was for this reason that the predecessors of s. 9 of the 1954 Act and s. 4 of the 1980 Act were enacted, to facilitate enforcement of the agreement to arbitrate.

---

19 [1930] IR 265.
20 Id. at p. 269.

SOURCES OF THE LAW

The principal source of the law of arbitration is the agreement of the parties, express and implied, to submit their differences to arbitration subject to the provisions of the arbitral legislation and the common law.

Statute There is no Continental European-style code of arbitration. The Arbitration Act, 1954, provides for several problems that tend to arise in arbitrations and sets out mechanisms through which the court can supervise the conduct of arbitrations. But there are many legal issues that arise which are not addressed by this Act; for instance, it provides no guidance on the numerous procedural problems that can arise in the course of a reference. As is explained below, where the arbitration is not the subject of an 'arbitration agreement' as defined by the 1954 Act, then that Act does not apply—most notably, where the agreement is not 'written'.

Discretions: Many of the 1954 Act's provisions confer a discretion on the court but do not indicate how that discretion is to be exercised; for instance, the power to revoke an arbitration agreement, to appoint and to remove arbitrators, to remit an award. In several instances in recent years the courts have stressed the extent of the discretion they possess under these provisions—on one occasion even rejecting a view held for nearly 100 years that the discretion to remit an award can only be exercised in several narrowly defined circumstances.[21]

Peremptory Nature: To what extent are the provisions of the 1954 Act peremptory—meaning compulsory, that is, apply to all arbitrations which are governed by Irish law and the parties cannot contract out of their requirements? This question has arisen in particular with regard to the sections enabling judicial supervision of the reference and review of any awards that are made. Can the parties by agreement exclude judicial review, or at least some forms of judicial review? The answer to this question has been no. In *Czarnikow v. Ross, Schmidt & Co.,*[22] the rules of a trade association governing arbitration between its members precluded either party from asking the arbitrator to state a special case to the High Court, which is the principal mode of judicial supervision provided for in the Arbitration Act. It was held that this clause was ineffective because it contravened public policy, since it purported to oust the jurisdiction of the courts over arbitrations. As was explained by Scrutton LJ,

21   *King v. Thomas McKenna Ltd* [1991] 2 QB 480; see post p. 126.
22   [1922] 2 KB 478.

to allow English citizens to agree to exclude this safeguard (i.e. the case stated procedure) for the administration of the law is contrary to public policy. There must be no Alsatia in England where the King's writ does run. . . . Without attempting precisely to define the limits within which an agreement not to take proceedings in the King's Courts is unenforceable, I think an agreement to shut out the power of the King's Courts to guide the proceedings of inferior tribunals without legal training in matters of law before them is calculated to lead to erroneous administration of law, and therefore injustice, and should therefore not be recognized by the Courts.[23]

It would seem, however, that this approach no longer has unqualified support, especially in arbitrations with a distinctive international element between legally sophisticated parties of equal bargaining power. For instance, one of the terms of the arbitration rules of the International Chamber of Commerce (ICC) is that the parties 'waive their right to any form of appeal' against an award, insofar as such waiver can be validly made.[24] The objective is to keep ICC awards outside of the courts to the extent that it is legally possible to do so. It was held by the New Zealand Court of Appeal in *CBI NZ Ltd. v. Badger Chiyoda*[25] that this clause did not offend against the present day public policy of New Zealand. And it was suggested there that the *Czarnikow* decision might not be followed today. In the case of big international arbitrations, a variety of reasons were given why, if anything, current public policy favours rather than discourages the exclusion of judicial review of an arbitrator's findings.

Agreement   The very source of an arbitrator's authority is the parties' agreement to resolve their dispute through the process of arbitration. Often, that agreement will also contain, or will be supplemented by, an agreement about how the reference is to be conducted. Frequently, the parties will select a model arbitration agreement published by a professional association, for instance the Irish branch of Chartered Instituted of Arbitrators' Rules.[26] Parties to an international arbitration may select the Rules of the International Chamber of Commerce[27] or the model 'UNCITRAL' Rules promulgated by the United Nations Commission on International Trade Law;[28] commodities arbitrations are frequently conducted under the 'GAFTA'

23   Id. at p. 488.
24   Art. 24(2).
25   [1989] 2 NZLR 669; see further, post p. 117.
26   Reproduced infra pp. 147 et seq.
27   Reproduced in *Mustill & Boyd*, pp. 743-763.
28   Reproduced in id. pp. 763-779.

Rules.[29] Indeed, there is a plethora of model arbitration rules from which disputants can choose. Often, parties will select a particular set of rules and make certain changes to them. Occasionally, the parties may initially sit down and agree on an entire set of arbitration rules and principles between themselves. Whether the applicable procedures are of the parties' own devising or are based on model rules, the legal basis for the entire procedure is a contract between the parties. Accordingly, many issues regarding the proper conduct of the arbitration can be resolved by straight-forward contract law analysis.

The contractual basis for the law of arbitration was stressed in the *Bremer Vulkan* case,[30] which concerned whether arbitrators are empowered to dismiss 'stale' arbitrations for want of prosecution, and this case is an excellent example of the application of ordinary contract law principles to resolve such questions. According to Lord Diplock, there is

> a fundamental difference between action at law and arbitration. . . . As plaintiff and defendant in an action, the parties assume no contractual obligations to one another as to what each must do in the course of the proceedings; their respective obligations as to procedure are imposed upon them by the rules and practice of the court. In contrast to this, the submission of a dispute to arbitration under a private arbitration agreement is purely voluntary by both claimant and respondent. Where the arbitration agreement is in a clause forming part of a wider contract and provides for the reference to arbitration of all future disputes arising under or concerning the contract, neither party knows when the agreement is entered into whether he will be claimant or respondent in disputes to which the arbitration agreement will apply.
> . . .
> In an arbitration there is no fixed pattern of procedure; what steps are to be taken by each party in a particular arbitration and the timetable which each party must observe are matters to be determined by the arbitrator. . . .
> By appointing a sole arbitrator pursuant to a private arbitration agreement which does not specify expressly or by reference any particular procedural rules, the parties make the arbitrator the master of the procedure to be followed in the arbitration. Apart from a few statutory requirements, . . . he has a complete discretion to determine

---

29   I.e. Grain & Food Trade Association Rules.
30   *Bremer Vulkan Schiffbau und Mischinenfabrik v. South India Shipping Corp.* [1982] AC 909.

how the arbitration is to be conducted from the time of his appointment to the time of his award, so long as the procedure he adopts does not offend the rules of natural justice.[31]

Common law and equity By common law and equity is meant the principles which guide the courts especially where the issue to be decided is not governed by statutory provisions or the express terms of a contract. Because statute leaves many matters unregulated and because often many matters are not addressed in the parties' agreement, the courts must devise solutions. Often this is done by implying certain terms into the parties' agreement; in the court's view, if the parties had actually addressed themselves to the issue, this is how they would have dealt with it. A term will then be impled into the contract to that effect.

While the courts allow the parties an extensive freedom regarding what they can agree on, it is not an unlimited freedom. Most notably, they cannot contract out of the supervisory powers which the 1954 Act confers on the courts, for instance, to remit or to set aside an award. As was stated above, however, in recent years and especially with reference to international arbitration agreements, the courts are beginning to tolerate some 'ouster of jurisdiction' clauses in arbitration agreements, for instance, article 24 in the ICC's arbitration rules.[32]

HISTORICAL CONTEXT

The first Irish Arbitration Act was adopted around the time the Treaty of Limerick was signed. The Act 'for determining differences by Arbitration' of 1698[33] was designed to render arbitration agreements more effective. Previously, the only way in which such agreements could be made enforceable by the courts was for the parties in dispute first to commence litigation and then apply to the court for the matter to be submitted to arbitration. The eventual award, therefore, was part of the judicial process and would be enforced as such. What the 1698 Act did was to make it no longer necessary to commence litigation for this purpose. Instead, if the contracting parties agreed that their arbitration clause should be made a rule of court, then the court would enforce the arbitrator's award as if it were a rule of court.

31 Id. at pp. 983, 984 and 985.
32 *CBI (NZ) Ltd v. Badger Chiyoda* [1989] 2 NZLR 669.
33 10 Wm. III c. 14.

A major weakness in the arbitration system was that a party could, with impunity, in effect flout his agreement to arbitrate a dispute. That could be done by him refusing to appoint an arbitrator—where, of course, he had a power of appointment. Or it could be done by him launching court proceedings about the dispute which ought to have been arbitrated. Courts would try the dispute, notwithstanding an arbitration clause, on the grounds that any contractual stipulation purporting to deny a court jurisdiction was contrary to public policy. In other words, arbitration agreements, even though not illegal, were unenforceable because they offended against the public policy that the courts have a monopoly of formal disputes—resolution. In the early nineteenth century judges' remuneration was determined by the number and value of cases they heard, which may have encouraged the application of this 'public policy' to arbitrations.

The House of Lords decision in *Scott v. Avery*[34] enormously encouraged arbitration, by endorsing a simple expedient for getting around the public policy principle. Instead of the parties simply agreeing to arbitrate their differences, they would agree that, before any court could address their differences, the matter must first be the subject of arbitration. In the *Scott* case, the formula used, to this end, was that no party 'shall be entitled to maintain any [legal proceedings] until the matters in dispute shall have been referred to, and decided by, arbitrators. . . .' The plaintiff there rejected an offer by the defendant and commenced proceedings. It was argued, for the defendant, that the above clause required resort to arbitration before a legal claim could be brought. But, it was argued, the arbitration clause contravened public policy because it purported to oust the jurisdiction of the courts. When the matter got to the House of Lords, the Law Lords summoned a panel of senior judges for their advice on the matter. By the narrowest of majorities, they advised that the clause did not offend against public policy and that view was unanimously endorsed by the Lords. By stipulating for arbitration before any litigation could commence, the courts' jurisdiction was not being ousted. Rather, litigation was merely being postponed until the arbitrators had their say in the matter. Until well into the present century, following this decision, many arbitration clauses were couched in a similar formula, known as '*Scott v. Avery* clauses'.[35]

This decision was given at a time when major reforms were being made in civil procedure in England and Ireland. Its pro-arbitration stance was fortified in the same year by s. 14 of the Common Law Procedure (Ireland) Act, 1856, which empowered courts to stay litigation where the subject

34   (1856) 5 HL Cas 811.
35   See *Mustill & Boyd* ch. 13.

matter of the dispute was covered by an arbitration clause, even one not in the *Scott v. Avery* mould. Therefore, once a dispute fell within the terms of an arbitration clause, the courts would refuse to accept seisin of that dispute and instead would insist that it go to arbitration, unless there were special reasons why the court should deal with the issues. This Act also introduced the 'case stated' procedure,[36] whereby issues could be referred from the arbitral tribunal to the High Court, and also the Court's power to remit an award back to the arbitrator to remedy some defect.[37]

The 1698 Act remained in force for over 250 years and, indeed, in 1946 Davitt J in the High Court[38] had to deal with various aspects of enforcing an arbitration through the rule of court procedure. Changes to the law introduced in England in 1889[39] were not extended to Ireland before the 1950s.

In 1954 the Oireachtas adopted the present Arbitration Act. When introducing the second stage of the Bill in the Dáil, the then Minister for Justice summarised its thrust as

> follow[ing] the system that obtains in England and the United States. The giving to the courts in England and in the United States of such large supervisory and controlling powers in arbitration cases has been the subject of adverse comment on the Continent where the powers of the courts with respect to arbitrations are generally more restricted and very precisely defined. The system of arbitration proposed in the Bill appears to have worked very well in England and, in framing our proposals, we have naturally taken into account the experience of a country which belongs to the same legal family. . . .[40]

There was little discussion of the Bill's provisions in the Dáil or the Seanad.

The Arbitration Act, 1980, was enacted in order to facilitate enforcement of arbitration awards under the New York (1958) and the Washington (1965) Conventions.[41] This 1980 Act altered the domestic arbitration rules in one significant respect, by making the power to stop parallel court proceedings a peremptory and not a discretionary power. Under s. 5 of the 1980 Act, stays of parallel court proceedings are no longer within the court's

---

36   S. 8; the power here to state a case is made subject to any agreement to the contrary.
37   S. 11.
38   *Re Elkinson & Doyle's Arbitration* [1946] IR 248, 464, 476.
39   Arbitration Act, 1889.
40   1954 Dáil Debates, Vol. 147, col. 294.
41   Reproduced in the schedules to that Act.

discretion but are compulsory or automatic. Some judges have indicated discomfort with this provision when they were faced with situations where, before 1980, a stay would not have been ordered. It has been suggested by some observers that this section may be unconstitutional; others have said that when faced with a situation where, in justice, the litigation should be allowed to proceed, the courts may hold that the arbitration clause itself was unconstitutionally obtained and, therefore, is unenforceable.

STATUTORY ARBITRATION ARRANGEMENTS

There are certain statutory arbitration systems where legislation requires or permits designated matters to be resolved by arbitration in accordance with specified procedures. Thus, where property is expropriated for some public purpose, the compensation payable is generally determined by arbitration under the Acquisition of Land (Assessment of Compensation) Act, 1919.[42] Where property is expropriated under the Minerals Development Acts, 1940-79, the procedures of the 1919 Act apply to the determination of the compensation, subject to certain qualifications.[43] Where shareholders who object to a company's restructuring under s. 260 of the Companies Act, 1963, want to have their shares bought by the company, in the absence of agreement the price is determined by arbitration under the Companies Clauses Consolidation Act, 1845.[44]

Most features of these statutory arbitrations are made subject to the 1954 Act. According to s. 48(2) of that Act,

> Parts I and II of this Act (except the excluded provisions) shall apply to every arbitration under any other Act as if the arbitration were pursuant to an arbitration agreement and as if that other Act were an arbitration agreement, except insofar as Part II of this Act is inconsistent with that other Act or with any rules or procedures authorised or recognised thereby.

The 'excluded provisions' of the 1954 Act, which do *not* apply to statutory arbitrations, are

s. 10(1)—death of party

s. 11—provisions in case bankruptcy

---

42 See generally, S. McDermott & R. Woulfe, *Compulsory Purchase and Compensation: Law and Practice in Ireland* (1992) ch. 8.
43 Minerals Development Act, 1940, s. 59.
44 Companies Act, 1963, s. 260(6).

s. 13—interpleader

s. 39—power of court to grant relief where arbitrator is not impartial or the dispute referred involves questions of fraud

s. 40—power of court where arbitrator in removed or authority is revoked

s. 45—power of court to extend time for commencing an arbitration

s. 46—extension of s.496 Merchant Shipping Act, 1894

Apart from the sections listed above, except where the 1954 Act is inconsistent with provisions of the Act authorising the statutory arbitration in question, that arbitration is subject to the 1954 Act as if there had been an arbitration agreement. Thus, for instance, in *Cmrs. of Public Works v. Flood*,[45] it was held that the 1954 Act's 'case stated' procedure applied to arbitration under the Arterial Drainage Act, 1945.

A matter that still has to be fully resolved is the relationship between judicial review under R.S.C. Order 84 and judicial supervision of statutory arbitrators under the 1954 Act's procedures.[46] In particular, can arbitrators' awards be challenged and set aside under Order 84 on grounds which would not succeed when seeking to challenge a consensual arbitration under the 1954 Act?

Where an arbitration clause in a contract refers to a statutory arbitration procedure which was designed for that type of dispute, then generally the arbitration will be regarded as statutory rather than exclusively within the 1954 Act. For instance,[47] where a commercial lease stated that disputes about rent shall be decided by the Lands Tribunal, it was held that all the provisions of the Act establishing that Tribunal applied, including that Act's provisions for judicial review of the Tribunal's determinations at the instigation of any 'person aggrieved'.

The legislation governing friendly societies and industrial and provident societies envisages arbitration of disputes between these societies and their members but do not actually require arbitration. Section 68 of the Friendly Societies Act, 1896, and s. 49 of the Industrial and Provident Societies Act, 1893, are similar. They state that disputes of this nature 'shall be decided in a manner directed by the rules of the society'. The rules of almost every one of these societies provide for arbitration of these disputes. Of course, there

---

45   [1980] ILRM 38.
46   Cf. *Manning v. Shackleton and Cork C.C.* [1944] ILRM 346 (an Order 84 application) and *Doyle v. Shackleton and Kildare C.C.* (Flood J, 20 January 1994) (brought under the 1954 Act).
47   *Antrim Newtown Developments Ltd v. Department of Environment* [1989] N.I. 26.

are certain kinds of disputes with these societies which fall outside such arbitration clauses.[48] These sections add that any dispute decided in accordance with a society's rules 'shall be binding and conclusive on all the parties without appeal, and shall not be removable into any court of law or restrainable by injunction'.[49] The extent to which these provisions effectively exclude all judicial review of these arbitrations does not seem to have been authoritatively discussed in recent years.

ARBITRATIONS OUTSIDE THE 1954 ACT

If the dispute-resolution machinery does not possess the characteristics summarised above[50] then the Arbitration Act, 1954, as amended, has no application to it. But that machinery may very well be an arbitration and it still may not be subject to the 1954 Act. There are three principal types of arbitration that fall outside the Act. Mention should also be made of Part IV of the 1954 Act, which authorises the Circuit Court, the High Court and even the Supreme Court to refer to an arbitrator certain issues which have arisen in litigation before the court.

Unwritten agreement   One is where the agreement to arbitrate is not 'written', as is required in the definition section of the 1954 Act. It would seem that the terms of the agreement do not have to be set out in any great detail in the document; it should suffice if it is clear from the document or from other documents to which it refers that the parties intended disputes of a particular nature to be arbitrated. There is no requirement that the document should be signed.

Jurisdiction enlarged informally   An arbitrator may be properly seized of a reference and the parties then informally agree that he should deal with some additional matters, not covered by their written agreement. In other words, the arbitrator's jurisdiction is extended by an informal *ad hoc* submission. For instance in *Royal Commission of Wheat Supplies v. Usher*,[51] which concerned a statutory arbitration directed by court order, the arbitrator was empowered to determine how much compensation should be paid for barley that was requisitioned during the war. During the course of

---

48   E.g. *Andrews v. Mitchell* [1905] AC 78 and *McEllistrim v. Ballymacelligot Co-Op*
     [1919] AC 548.
49   1896 Act s.68(1) and 1893 Act s.49(1).
50   Supra pp. 4 et seq.
51   [1920] 2 IR 483.

the reference, the parties made a voluntary submission that the arbitrator should also 'deal with all differences incidental thereto and also with the costs.' One of the parties sought judicial review of the award in relation to these additional matters. It was held that, while there would be no legal objection to the parties extending the authority of the statutory arbitrator, his determinations on those matters were outside the Arbitration Act and, accordingly, were not reviewable under its provisions.

Another somewhat exceptional instance is where the parties agree, even in writing, that the arbitrator should determine an issue concerning the existence of the underlying contract.

Labour arbitration   Arbitration has a central role in the labour laws of several large industrialised countries and there is an abundance of case law on the operation of those labour arbitration systems. The position in Ireland is very different except for the public sector. In the private sector here, it would seem that arbitration clauses in individual employment contracts and in collective agreements are virtually unheard of. Even if such agreements did contain arbitration clauses, serious doubts exist about their legal efficacy, on account of s. 5(a) of the Arbitration Act, 1954.

Section 5(a)   According to s. 5(a) of the 1954 Act,

> Notwithstanding anything contained in this Act, this Act does not apply to an arbitration under an agreement providing for any references to, or settlement by, arbitration *of any question relating to the terms of conditions of employment or the remuneration of any employees*, including persons employed by or under the State or local authorities. (italics supplied)

The principal reason for enacting s. 5(a) was to prevent institutionalised labour arbitration being made subject to judicial review in the High Court. Several of the provisions of the 1954 Act provide for judicial review of arbitration, either during the conduct of the reference or after the reference— for instance, to stop the reference, to remove the arbitrator, the consultative case stated, directions for a special case and an application for redress because of the arbitrator's misconduct of the reference. Unless the 1954 Act was made inapplicable, all of these review mechanisms would apply to labour arbitration.

One form of arbitration is expressly referred to in s. 5(b) of that Act, viz. arbitration by the Labour Court, with the consent of all the parties involved, of a 'trade dispute' which has occurred or is apprehended. Another form of arbitration the Oireachtas clearly had in mind was arbitration arrangements in the public sector—the forerunners of the present Schemes for Conciliation and Arbitration for civil servants, for teachers, for personnel in An Post and Bord Telecom Éireann, for officers of local authorities and of health authorities and for members of the Garda Síochána.[52] In 1948 the in-coming Coalition Government declared that they favoured regulating industrial relations in the civil service through arbitration. A trial scheme was established in 1950, although it was suspended in controversial circumstances in 1952. The present civil service scheme was adopted in 1955.

According to the Minister opening the second reading of the Bill in the Dáil, on 3 November 1954:

> Section 5 excludes arbitrations under agreements relating to the terms and conditions of employment. These are not arbitrations properly so called at all as the arbitrator has no power to make a final enforceable award, nor do the parties to the arbitration intend in any way that he should. The section specifically excludes arbitration under section 70 of the Industrial Relations Act 1946, which empowers the Labour Court, with the consent of the parties, to refer an actual or apprehended trade dispute to arbitration. Arbitration dealing with conditions of employment and trade disputes are really informal matters and it was decided that it should be made quite clear that the Bill was not to apply to them. If the proposed legislation did apply, these arbitrations would have to be carried out in accordance with formal rules, and the law as to the swearing of witnesses, discovery of documents, costs, removal of the arbitrator by the High Court, etc., would apply to them. I think everybody will agree that such arbitrations, if they can be properly so called, should not be treated in this manner. The arbitrators are really mediators who make recommendations and it is up to the parties to accept these recommendations or not to accept them as they so think fit.[53]

Employment contracts   Does s. 5(a) of the 1954 Act apply to (and therefore exclude) arbitration clauses contained in individual employment contracts? The answer would seem to be no. From the Oireachtas debates, it does not appear that the section was intended to exclude such clauses in these contracts. If, as in some countries, it was intended to protect employees from being tied by arbitration clauses, s. 5(a) would simply have stated that position in clear terms; as it is shown below, the non-application of the 1954 Act would not mean that the arbitration clause is a complete nullity. Also,

52   See generally, M. Forde, *Industrial Relations Law* (1991), pp. 200-206.
53   Dáil Debates, Vol. 147, cols 297-298.

the reference in s. 5(a) is to the 'terms etc. of employees'; it is in the plural, suggesting arbitration clauses that apply to two or more employees and not a clause affecting just one employee only.

Some union-employer disputes   It is not every dispute arising under a collective agreement that is affected by s. 5(a) of the 1954 Act. What is taken outside the Arbitration Acts are disputes about 'any question relating to the terms and conditions of employment or the remuneration of any employees'. Some disputes which arise between trade unions and employers do not directly concern employees' 'pay or their terms or conditions of employment'. The key phrase is 'relating to'. Will it be given an expansive or restrictive interpretation? Most likely it will be interpreted along the same lines as the so-called 'golden formula'—the definition of what is a 'trade dispute', now in s. 8 of the Industrial Relations Act, 1990.[54] Over the years the courts have construed the phrase 'connected with' employment etc. in that definition more expansively.

For reasons of consistency it is suggested that the criteria for determining whether a dispute is 'connected with' employment etc., in the trade dispute context should govern this question in arbitration. If this approach is adopted, then the leading modern authority would be the Northern Ireland decision. *Crazy Prices (N.I.) Ltd. v. Hewitt*,[55] where the immediate cause of the dispute was selling bread at bottom-of-the-market prices. Under this approach, arbitrating disputes about, for example, union recognition, subcontracting work, shut-downs, fringe benefits and at times pension entitlements would not be affected by the Arbitration Acts.

Outside the Arbitration Acts   Putting certain categories of disputes outside the Arbitration Acts does not mean that those disputes can never be the subject of arbitration and that any arbitrations of such disputes that may take place are complete nullities. However, the precise legal status of these arbitrations is something of a puzzle. Mustill & Boyd just touch on the subject, with regard to arbitrations which are not subject to an 'arbitration agreement', as defined in the Arbitration Acts, and, therefore, entirely beyond the scope of those Acts. The learned authors comment that '[t]hese references will, however, continue to be subject to the fast-developing powers of the court at common law to supervise consensual arbitration'.[56] The following observations suggest what the legal position might be.

It can hardly be doubted that the automatic stay on parallel court

54   Supra n.52, pp. 125-146.
55   [1980] NI 150; see id. pp. 131-132.
56   *Commercial Arbitration*, at p. 51.

proceedings, contained in s. 5 of the Arbitration Act, 1980,[57] would not apply. Since, however, the parties opted for arbitration, it is probable that the courts would exercise their discretion to stay parallel proceedings, unless there are good reasons for allowing the civil action to proceed.[58] In England the power to stay proceedings where the parties have agreed to arbitration is discretionary except for international disputes, where it is compulsory. In *Goodman v. Winchister & Alton plc*[59] the plaintiff was employed as general manager under a contract of employment. At the suggestion of the plaintiff's solicitor when negotiations for the contract were becoming protracted, a clause was added requiring every dispute or difference arising between the parties to be referred to arbitration. Following complaints relating to the plaintiff's performance of his duties, he was summarily dismissed. He subsequently obtained other employment but at a greatly reduced salary. With the assistance of legal aid, he commenced proceedings for damages for wrongful dismissal. The company applied to stay the proceedings pursuant to s. 4 of the (English) Arbitration Act, 1950. The trial judge found that the parties had not contemplated that the arbitration clause would apply to summary dismissal and he refused a stay on the ground that the plaintiff could not afford to arbitrate, his poverty on the face of it being caused by the defendant's alleged breach of contract. It was held by the Court of Appeal that, in exercising its discretion whether to grant a stay of judicial proceedings under the Arbitration Act 1950, the financial position of the plaintiff was a relevant but not a decisive factor. On the evidence, in particular that the plaintiff was responsible for the inclusion of the arbitration clause in the contract of employment, the plaintiff's poverty, thought alleged to have been induced by a breach of contract by the defendant, was not sufficient to displace the court's *prima facie* duty under s. 4 to hold parties to their agreement to arbitrate.

Provided the reference was conducted properly, there is no reason in principle why the courts should not enforce the award against the party who lost. The argument for enforcement is that an award was envisaged in the contract and, unless the clause stipulated that there was to be non-binding arbitration, it is an implied term (based on the 'efficacy' principle) that the award would be enforceable.

Finally and perhaps most controversially, there is the question of the extent to which the award will be subject to judicial review. Again, presumably the courts would intervene if there was manifest departure from fair procedures, for instance fraud and bias, and, as they have done for centuries

57   See ch. 2.
58   Cf. *Channel Tunnel Group v. Balfour Beatty Ltd* [1993] AC 334.
59   [1985] 1 WLR 141.

in all arbitrations, where there is an error of law on the face of the record. In *Jones v. Sherwood Computer Services plc*,[60] the Court of Appeal laid down the circumstances where it would upset a determination made by a party acting as a valuer and not an arbitrator. The question then is, where he is acting as arbitrator but is outside the 1954 Act, how much more intensively will the courts scrutinise the award and how it was reached.

PROSCRIBED ARBITRATIONS

The laws of several countries do not permit certain matters to be arbitrated; indeed at one time the French courts, perhaps jealous of their jurisdiction under the *Code Civil*, regarded all arbitration clauses as unlawful, except clauses in international agreements.[61] Arbitration has since become acceptable almost universally and prohibitions against resolving certain matters by arbitration are exceptional. But the French Labour Code prohibits this method of resolving disputes between parties to a contract of employment.[62] There are no such provisions in Irish law; perhaps the nearest is s. 5 of the 1954 Act which renders that Act inapplicable to certain kinds of labour arbitration.

A question which has arisen at times is whether certain statutory provisions that confer rights, which do not mention the question of arbitration, permit the determination of those rights by arbitrators. This matter has been before the United States Supreme Court in recent years on several occasions, where the issue was whether courts should enforce agreements to arbitrate disputes about several statutory rights and duties—for instance under the Securities Exchange Act,[63] which regulates stocks exchange dealings, under the Sherman Act,[64] which outlaws various anti-competitive practices, and under the anti-racketeering 'RICO' law.[65] Formerly, such agreements were condemned as being against public policy but, since the *Mitsubishi Motors* case in 1985,[66] the Court has enthusiastically endorsed arbitration of international and even domestic commercial disputes concerning statutory claims. On the other hand, agreements to arbitrate disputes arising out of labour or civil rights legislation continue being disregarded

---

60   [1992] 1 WLR 277.
61   Cf. *Hecht v. Soc. Buisman's*, Cour d'App. Paris, 19 June 1970 [1971] RCDIP 692; Cass. Civ. 4 July 1972 [1974] RCDIP 82.
62   Code du Travail art. R.517-1; e.g. *Motokov v. Semeriva*, Cass. Soc. 9 December 1960 [1961] J-CP I, 12029.
63   *Scherk v. Alberto Culver Co.*, 417 US 506 (1974).
64   *Mitsubishi Motors Corp. v. Soler Chrysler-Plymouth Inc.*, 473 US 614 (1985).
65   *Shearson American Express Inc. v. McMahon*, 482 US 220 (1987).
66   Supra n.64; Cf. *Attorney General v. Mobil Oil NZ Ltd* [1989] 2 NZLR 649.

for reasons of public policy[67]—that individuals cannot waive their entitlement to have disputes, concerning matters in which the public have a special interest, decided in the courts.

So far this question does not seem to have been addressed by the Irish courts. In *McCarthy v. Joe Walsh Tours Ltd.*[68] the court refused to stay parallel litigation, notwithstanding that there was an arbitration clause, because it was held that some of the clause's provisions contravened ss. 39 and 40 of the Sale of Goods and Supply of Services Act, 1980. Under these sections, where goods or services have been sold or supplied to a consumer, exclusion of liability in respect of those goods or services is prohibited. In this instance the plaintiff had purchased a package holding from the defendants and disputes arising from that holiday were subject to the Irish Travel Agents' Association arbitration scheme. In the arbitration clause it was stated that the scheme '*inter alia* limits the liability of the company' in the manner set out in the Association's scheme—being a ceiling of £5,000 in any claim and excluding liability for personal injury. By virtue of this attempted exclusion, Carroll J held that the arbitration clause contravened ss. 39 and 40 of the 1980 Act and, therefore, was ineffective. It would seem, however, that the arbitration here should have been allowed to take place, but with the clear statement that the arbitrator is not bound by the stated limitation on liability, which the 1980 Act proscribes. Strictly, the purported limitation has nothing to do with arbitration. Perhaps the court here was indicating its dislike of arbitration clauses in contracts between parties who were in apparent unequal bargaining positions.

67   E.g. *Alexander v. Gardner Denver Co.*, 415 US 36 (1974).
68   [1991] ILRM 813.

2

STAYS ON PARALLEL LITIGATION

It is a general principle of contract law that the courts will not enforce a clause in an agreement to oust the jurisdiction of the courts.[1] Generally, such 'ouster' clauses are regarded as contrary to public policy. In a trade union discipline case,[2] for example, where one of the union's rules stipulated that aggrieved members of the union had to exhaust all domestic remedies before they could resort to litigation, that rule was held to contravene public policy. In the past, one of the justifications given for judicial hostility to arbitration clauses was that they purported to oust the jurisdiction of the courts.[3] Accordingly, the courts would permit parties to litigate their disputes notwithstanding that they came within the terms of an arbitration clause. As was explained earlier, when arbitration arrangements became somewhat more acceptable to the judiciary, an exception was made for one type of arbitration provision, the *Scott v. Avery* clause. If arbitration was provided for as a prerequisite to any litigation, then the parties have not agreed to exclude the courts entirely from hearing their dispute. Most arbitration clauses, therefore, in the latter part of the nineteenth century and at the beginning of this century adopted the *Scott v. Avery* formula.

An ordinary arbitration clause is not a contract to oust the court's jurisdiction and, with one qualification, the parties to such clauses are not thereby prevented from prosecuting their claims in court rather than by arbitration. However, for arbitration agreements within the 1954-1980 Acts, a party can be easily prevented from prosecuting his claim in court if it relates to an issue covered by the arbitration clause. Prior to 1980, the court had discretion as to whether parallel proceedings should be stayed.[4] If the party seeking the stay was 'ready and willing' to arbitrate and there was no other 'sufficient reason' why the dispute should not be resolved in that manner, a stay would be granted; there was a considerable body of case law on the considerations governing the decision to order a stay. If, for instance,

1 A.G. Guest, ed., *Chitty on Contracts* (26th ed. 1989) vol. 1, pp. 708 et seq.
2 *Leigh v. National Union of Railwaymen* [1970] Ch. 326.
3 See ante p. 12.
4 1954 Act s. 12(1), originally the Common Law Procedure Amendment Act (Ireland), 1856, s. 14; see *Mustill & Boyd*, pp. 466-483.

the arbitrator was not a lawyer but a decision on a question of law went 'to the root of the whole inquiry', a court was inclined to refuse a stay.[5] Similarly, if an allegation of fraud was central to the action being brought, the tendency was not to grant a stay.[6]

MANDATORY STAYS

This discretion was taken away by s. 5(1) of the Arbitration Act, 1980, which states

> If any party to an arbitration agreement, or any person claiming through or under him, commences any proceedings in any court against any other party to such agreement, or any person claiming through or under him, in respect of any matter agreed to be referred to arbitration, any party to the proceedings may at any time after an appearance has been entered, and before delivering any pleadings or taking any other steps in the proceedings, apply to the court to stay the proceedings, and the court, unless it is satisfied that the arbitration agreement is null and void, inoperative or incapable of being performed or that there is not in fact any dispute between the parties with regard to the matter agreed to be referred, shall make an order staying the proceedings.

Now provided the dispute which a party is seeking to litigate falls within the scope of an enforceable arbitration agreement he made, on the application of the other party, the court will direct that those proceedings shall be stayed.[7] Although the 1980 Act deals almost entirely with foreign arbitrations, s. 5 applies as much to domestic as to foreign arbitration agreements. Whether the court should have been deprived of all discretion in this matter is debatable; circumstances can arise where it may be more just and convenient to permit the litigation to go ahead. Where, however, the party who obtained a stay then unduly delays in carrying on with the reference, the court may conclude that he has abandoned the arbitration agreement and, consequently, it may decide to lift the stay.[8]

Parallel proceedings being brought in a foreign court do not fall within s. 5 of the 1980 Act. However, the High Court has inherent jurisdiction to

5   *Hogg v. Belfast Corp.* [1919] 2 IR 305.
6   *Workman v. Belfast Harbour Comrs.* [1899] 2 IR 234.
7   *Williams v. Artane Service Station Ltd* [1991] ILRM 893 and *Sweeney v. Mulcahy* [1993] ILRM 289.
8   *O'Mahony v. Lysaght* [1988] IR 29.

enjoin a party from continuing such proceedings.[9]

Prerequisites for a stay In order to obtain a stay under s. 5, the following must be established. An enforceable arbitration agreement must exist between the applicant seeking the stay and the party to the court proceedings or a party who is claiming through him. The parallel proceedings in question must be being brought in a court, not in an administrative or quasi-judicial tribunal or in another arbitration. Those proceedings must have commenced; a premature application for a stay will be refused. And the claim being made in the proceedings must be one which is covered by the arbitration agreement. The question is whether the claim, as formulated in the writ or pleadings, is one which could have been arbitrated. Thus, where Belfast Corporation sued a builder for not constructing houses,[10] under an agreement made in early 1914, which undertaking was delayed on account of the outbreak of war, it was held that the central issue in the dispute, that of the effect of that delay on the contract, did not fall within the terms of the arbitration agreement and, accordingly, the court action could not be stayed. Where a party obtained third party insurance against losses caused by a lift which was installed,[11] and all claims under the policy were to be submitted to arbitration, an action for damages to the lift itself was held not to fall within the agreement.

Where proceedings are being brought outside the High Court, such as in the District Court or in the Circuit Court, can those courts stay the action or must an application be brought in the High Court? Under s. 12 of the 1954 Act, which gave a discretionary power to stay, until repealed in 1980, the application could be made to 'that court', that is, the court where the proceedings were being brought. But s.5 of the 1980 Act says that the application should be brought in 'the Court' as the High Court. In *Mitchell v. Budget Travel Ltd*,[12] the Supreme Court held that the court in which the case is listed can stay the proceedings.

Person claiming through or under a party The authority of the court to stay parallel proceedings between parties to an arbitration clause extends to persons who are 'claiming through or under' either of the parties. This phrase has been held to apply to, for instance, a trustee of a bankrupt's

---

9 *Pena Copper Mines Ltd v. Rio Tinto Co.* (1911) 105 LT 846 and *Aggeliki Charis Co. Maritima S.A. v. Pagnan Spa* [1994] 1 LlLR 168.
10 Supra n. 5.
11 *Northern Publishing Office (Belfast) Ltd v. Cornhill Insurance Co.* [1956] N.I. 157; see also *O'Connor v. Norwich Union Fire & Life Ins. Soc.* [1894] 2 IR 723.
12 [1990] ILRM 739.

estate;[13] an assignee of a debt arising out of a contract containing an arbitration clause;[14] a subsidiary company where the parent was a party to the arbitration agreement;[15] a parent company where its subsidiary is a party to the arbitration agreement when claims are brought against both companies based on the same facts.[16]

In *Tanning Research Labs. Inc. v. O'Brien*,[17] where the question was whether, in dealing with proofs of a debt, a company's liquidator fits the above description, the rationale of the principle was explained as follows:

> the prepositions 'through' and 'under' convey the notion of a derivative cause of action or ground of defence, that is to say, a cause of action or ground of defence derived from the party. In other words, an essential element of the cause of action or defence must be or must have been vested in or exercisable by the party before the person claiming through or under the party can rely on the cause of action or ground of defence. A liquidator may be a person claiming through or under a company because the causes of action or grounds of defence on which he relies are vested in or exercisable by the company; a trustee in bankruptcy may be such a person because the causes of action or grounds of defence on which he relies were vested in or exercisable by the bankrupt.
>
> A liquidator who defends his rejection of a proof of debt on the ground that, under the general law, the liability to which the proof relates is not enforceable against the company takes his stand on a ground which is available to the company. A liquidator who resists a claim made by a creditor against the assets available for distribution on the ground that there is no liability under the general law thus stands in the same position *vis-à-vis* the creditor as does the company. If the creditor and the company are bound by an international arbitration agreement applicable to the claim, there is no reason why the claim should not be determined as between the creditor and the liquidator in the same way as it would have been determined had no winding up been commenced. To exclude from the scope of an international arbitration agreement binding on a company matters between the other party to that agreement and the company's liquidator would give such

13   *Piercy v. Young* (1879) 14 ChD 200.
14   *Rumpit (Panama) SA v. Islamic Shipping Lines* [1984] 2 LIR 259.
15   *Roussel-Uclaf v. G.D. Searle & Co.* [1978] 1 Ll 225; compare *Mount Cook (Northland) Ltd v. Swedish Motors Ltd* [1986] 1 NZLR 720.
16   *J.J. Ryan & Sons v. Rhone Poulen Textile SA*, 863 F 2d 315 (1988). See generally, 'Arbitration Agreements and Groups of Companies', 27 *Int'l Lawyer* 941 (1993).
17   64 ALJLR 211 (1990).

agreements an uncertain operation and would jeopardise orderly arrangements.[18]

Steps in the proceedings   If the party seeking the stay has taken steps in the court proceedings, his application for a stay will be refused. As O'Hanlon J explained in *McCormac Products Ltd. v. Monaghan Co-op Ltd*,

> a party to an arbitration agreement is put to his election to proceed on foot of that agreement, or to concur in a resort to court proceedings to determine disputes, and if he takes steps which may be regarded as invoking the aid of the court he may well find that he has burned his boats if the other party to the arbitration agreement prefers to retain the matter in court instead of going back to arbitration. It can hardly be intended that a party seeking to enforce his contractual rights in a situation where the contract contains an arbitration clause, should be entitled to conduct the two forms of proceeding in tandem, extracting from the High Court such relief as it may be open to him to obtain at arbitration, while resorting to the arbitrator for concurrent rights under the contract.[19]

It was held there that, since the applicant had obtained an interim injunction against the other party contravening the agreement, disputes arising from which were to be arbitrated, he had elected for litigation and, consequently, was not entitled to a stay.

But a mere application to stay the proceedings could not be regarded as 'taking a step' in them for these purposes. Nor is filing an appearance or consenting to an adjournment such a step.[20] What is required is conduct which shows that the party has decided to use the courts to advance his case against the other party. The test laid down by Finlay P in *O'Flynn v. Bord Gais*[21] is whether the action taken involves costs which are lost when the matter is referred to arbitration—'in other words, a step which involves the jurisdiction of the court at this instance or which institutes some matter whether by way of motion or otherwise in the court. Generally 'the court should lean in favour of staying the proceedings.'[22] There, the defendant wrote to the plaintiff's solicitor seeking an extension of time to enter its defence. That was held not to be a step in the proceedings for these purposes. By contrast, in *Turner & Goudy v. McConnell*,[23] where summary proceed-

18   Id. at p. 215.
19   [1988] IR 304, at p.306.
20   *Air Nauru v. Niue Airlines Ltd* [1993] 2 NZLR 632.
21   [1982] ILRM 324.
22   Id. at p.325.

ings to recover a debt were commenced, the defendant filed an affidavit in opposition and appeared in the Master's Court, which caused the matter then to be listed for a hearing. That action, it was held, was a sufficient step for these purposes, and it did not matter when the step was taken that the party did not realise there was an arbitration clause or that he would have been entitled to obtain a stay.

DISCRETIONARY STAYS

The courts have a certain inherent jurisdiction to stay legal proceedings in particular circumstances where a defendant would suffer injustice by the action against him being continued. For instance, where parties to a dispute had agreed it should be decided by a foreign court, but one of them then brought proceedings in Ireland, the courts here would tend to stay that action until proceedings had been concluded in the chosen jurisdiction.[24] On analogy with this principle, in *Channel Tunnel Group v. Balfour Beatty Ltd*,[25] it was held that where parties have chosen some disputes-resolution procedure which strictly is not arbitration under the Arbitration Acts, the courts have an inherent power to stay parallel litigation of those disputes by either of the parties.

In this case, the disputes-resolution procedure chosen by the parties required the matter to be submitted first to experts and thereafter to arbitration. If this was an arbitration agreement, as defined, then clearly the mandatory stay would apply. It was held that this bi-furcated procedure was an arbitration. Even if it were not, it was held that, in the circumstances there, the court should exercise its inherent power to stay an action brought by one of the parties, concerning the price to be paid for variations of work done on the Channel Tunnel. The parties were large commercial organisations, with long experience in major commercial contracts, negotiating at arms length and familiar with the types of disputes arising in construction projects and the means for dealing with them. Having chosen this particular disputes-resolution procedure, they should be held to the terms of their agreement unless there were special reasons why that procedure should not be invoked. No such reasons were established here.

23   [1985] 1 WLR 898.
24   See generally, W. Binchy, *Irish Conflict of Laws* (1988) at pp. 162 et seq.
25   [1993] AC 334.

3

THE ARBITRATION AGREEMENT

The very basis for arbitration is an agreement between the parties to a dispute to submit it to arbitration. Unless the dispute in question is the subject of such an agreement, a person purporting to arbitrate it has no legal authority to do so.[1] Accordingly, one of the first things an arbitrator will do is to ascertain whether the matter being submitted for his decision is so covered. Most arbitration agreements contemplate future disputes, that is, disputes not existing at the time the agreement was made but which will or may arise in the future. There also can be *ad hoc* submissions to arbitration. Ordinarily any such agreement or submission does not affect third-parties.

EXISTENCE OF AN AGREEMENT

For the purpose of the 1954-1980 Acts, the parties must have concluded a written agreement to resolve their disputes in this manner; if no such contract has come into existence then the purported arbitrator has no authority at all to deal with the matter. As is explained below, in this regard arbitrators possess what is termed *kompetenz kompetenz* to some extent.

Type of contract   The agreement may deal exclusively with the question of arbitration, that is, the kinds of dispute which can be so determined, who shall adjudicate on them and the procedures to be followed. More often, however, the arbitration clause will be just one provision in a lengthy contract between the parties—be it a contract to sell property, to do work, build a bridge or a dam, or whatever. The articles of association of registered companies (which is a contract between the shareholders and their company and also a contract between the shareholders *inter se*) often provide for arbitration,[2] usually to determine the price of shares to be offered to shareholders for purchase.

1   *Porter v. Porter*, 55 ILTR 206 (1921) and *Hogan v. Poland* [1940] Ir Jur Rep 4.
2   Cf. *Beattie v. Beattie* [1938] 1 Ch 708.

Incorporation by reference   It is not essential that the agreement should contain the actual arbitration clause. It suffices if the contract refers to such a clause, which is somewhere else, in a way that the clause is incorporated into the contract.[3] Often the rules of a trade association regarding the terms on which its members deal with each other will contain arbitration provisions. It then generally suffices if the writing stipulates that the parties are contracting in accordance with the rules of a designated association, which posses such a clause.

But it is not always clear that an arbitration procedure was incorporated by reference, for instance, where goods are shipped and the bill of lading incorporates the charterparty, which contains an arbitration clause. Does that incorporate the charterparty arbitration procedure into the bill of lading? It has been held that, ordinarily, those terms of a charterparty which can be referentially incorporated into a bill of lading concern the conditions under which the goods are to be carried and delivered, and not collateral matters such as arbitration arrangements.[4] An arbitration clause which provides for arbitration 'in the usual way' or equivalent terms suffices if there indeed exists a usual mode of arbitration in the circumstances.

Certainty   As with all types of contracts, the arbitration agreement must be sufficiently certain to be enforced. Where there is some degree of uncertainty, the court will strive to carry out the very likely wishes of the parties. Depending on the circumstances, the mere words 'arbitrate' or 'arbitration' may suffice, where the meaning is clear.

SCOPE OF AGREEMENT

Whether any particular dispute is subject to arbitration depends on the very wording of the arbitration clause in question. For instance, a clause recommended by the Chartered Institute of Arbitrators states that

> Any dispute or difference of any kind whatsoever which arises or occurs between the parties in relation to any thing or matter arising under out of or in connection with this agreement shall be referred to arbitration under the Arbitration Rules of the Chartered Institute of Arbitrators.

And a clause recommended by the International Chamber of Commerce stipulates that

3   *Sweeney v. Mulcahy* [1993] ILRM 289.
4   *Skips A/S Nordheim v. Syrian Petroleum Co.* [1984] QB 599 and *Federal Bulk Carriers Inc. v. C. Ioth & Co.* [1989] 1 LILR 103.

All disputes arising in connection with the present contract shall be finally settled by arbitration.

The arbitration shall be held at .... and conducted in accordance with the Rules of (Conciliation and)* Arbitration of the International Chamber of Commerce.

The arbitration clause in the standard-form contract for the construction industry (the 'JCT Contract') states as follows

Article 5

If any dispute or difference as to the construction of this contract or any matter or thing of whatsoever nature arising thereunder or in connection therewith shall arise between the Employer or the Architect on his behalf and the Contractor either during the progress or after the completion or abandonment of the Works or after the determination of the employment of the Contractor, except under clause 31 (statutory tax deduction scheme) to the extent provided on clause 31.9. or under clause 3 of the VAT Agreement, it shall be and is hereby referred to arbitration in accordance with clause 41.

Part 4: Clause 41.1

When the Employer or the Contractor require a dispute or difference as referred to in Article 5 including:

> any matter or thing left by this contract to the discretion of the Architect, or
> the withholding by the Architect of any certificate to which the Contractor may claim to be entitled, or
> the adjustment of the Contract Sum under clause 30.6.2, or
> the rights and liabilities of the parties under clauses 27, 28, 32 or 33, or
> unreasonable withholding of consent or agreement by the Employer or the Architect on his behalf or by the Contractor

to be referred to arbitration then either the Employer or the Contractor shall give written notice to the other to such effect and such dispute or difference shall be referred to the arbitration and final decision of a person to be agreed between the parties as the Arbitrator, or, upon failure so to agree within 14 days after the date of the aforesaid written notice, of a person to be appointed as the Arbitrator on the request of either the Employer or the Contractor by the person named in the Appendix.

Especially where the reference will not be conducted under a set of institutional rules, the clause may add stipulations regarding, for example, the location and law of arbitration, time limits, exclusion of expert evidence, documents-only procedures, appointing an assessor and costs.

There are many reported decisions on the meaning of the particular forms of words which are commonly used in arbitration clauses, for instance, the words 'claims', 'differences', 'in connection with', 'in relation to', 'in respect of', 'with regard to', 'arising out of', 'under' and 'during the execution of'. The authoritative force of decisions construing a form of words in one contract is at most persuasive when those words are used in a different contract. This important point is well illustrated in *Ashville Investments Ltd v. Elmer Contractors*,[5] where the general approach to construing arbitration clauses was explained as follows:

> In seeking to construe a clause in a contract, there is no scope for adopting either a liberal or a narrow approach, whatever that may mean. The exercise which has to be undertaken is to determine what the words used mean. It can happen that in doing so one is driven to the conclusion that that clause is ambiguous, that it has two possible meanings. In those circumstances the court has to prefer one above the other in accordance with settled principles. If one meaning is more in accord with what the court considers to be the underlying purpose and intent of the contract, or part of it, than the other, then the court will choose the former rather than the latter. In some circumstances the court may reach its conclusion on construction by applying the *contra proferentem* rule. These are, however, well recognised principles of construction; they are not the consequences or examples of adopting any particular approach to the question of construction, save to ascertain the true intention of the parties and the correct meaning of the words used. . . .
>
> [I]t is a principle of law that the scope of an arbitrator's jurisdiction and powers in a given case depend fundamentally upon the terms of the arbitration agreement, that is to say upon its proper construction in all the circumstances. However, . . . there is [no] principle of law to the effect that the meaning of certain specific words in one arbitration clause in one contract is immutable and that those same specific words in another arbitration clause in other circumstances in another contract must be construed in the same way. This is not to say that the earlier decision on a given form of words will not be persuasive, to a degree dependent on the extent of the similarity between the contracts and

5   [1989] QB 488.

surrounding circumstances in the two cases. In the interests of certainty and clarity a court may well think it right to construe words in an arbitration agreement, or indeed in a particular type of contract, in the same way as those same words have earlier been construed in another case involving an arbitration clause by another court. But in my opinion the subsequent court is not bound by the doctrine of *stare decisis* to do so.[6]

Assuming the very terms of the arbitration clause are sufficiently wide to cover them, there are certain general issues which may lie beyond the competence of the arbitral tribunal.

The existence of the contract   This is one aspect of the vexed *kompetenz kompetenz* question, that is, the extent to which the arbitrator is authorised to determine his own jurisdiction.[7] Although arbitrators almost invariably at the outset will seek to satisfy themselves that a valid arbitration agreement exists, their decision on this point is not conclusive. Where, therefore, it seems that there could be a case for saying that there is no such agreement, the prudent thing for an arbitrator to do may be not to proceed any further until this vital prerequisite has been resolved by the parties, by them going to court and obtaining a declaration whether an enforceable agreement exists in the circumstances. It is a fundamental principle that the arbitrator has no authority to make a binding award as to the initial existence of the agreement from which his entire authority derives.

As Simon LC explained in *Heyman v. Darwins Ltd,*

An arbitration clause is a written submission, agreed to by the parties to the contract, and . . . must be construed according to its language and in the light of the circumstances in which it is made. If the dispute is whether the contract which contains the clause has ever been entered into at all, that issue cannot go to arbitration under the clause, for the party who denies that he has ever entered into the contract is thereby denying that he has ever joined in the submission. Similarly, if one party to the alleged contract is contending that it is void *ab initio* (because, for example, the making of such a contract is illegal), the arbitration clause cannot operate, for on this view the clause itself also is void.[8]

6   Id. at p. 494-495.
7   Cf. A. Redfern & M. Hunter, *Law and Practice of International Commercial Arbitration* (2nd ed. 1991) at pp. 275-280.
8   [1942] AC 356, at p. 366.

In other words, if in truth no contract was ever made, then the arbitration clause in the supposed contract can never have bound the parties and an arbitrator supposedly appointed under that clause can have no authority to act. This principle applies to issues such as the parties' lack of consensus, mistake, want of consideration, uncertainty.

The continued existence of the contract   One might think that, as a matter of logic, if an arbitrator lacks authority to determine whether or not the underlying contract ever came into existence then, he equally is disabled from making a binding ruling on whether the contract has come to an end, before the reference ever commenced. The first question, of course, is whether the very terms of the arbitration clause purport to confer such authority. Where the terms do so, there was uncertainty for decades about this question of competence.

The matter was resolved in the affirmative in *Heyman v. Darwins Ltd*,[9] where it was claimed that a party to an export sales contract, which contained an arbitration clause, had repudiated the contract. If the contract was indeed repudiated, it was argued, there no longer was authority to have disputes between the parties resolved by arbitration. That contention was rejected. As Lord Macmillan reasoned,

> an arbitration clause in a contract . . . is quite distinct from the other clauses. The other clauses set out the obligations which the parties undertake towards each other . . . but the arbitration clause does not impose on one of the parties an obligation in favour of the other. It embodies the agreement of both parties that, if any dispute arises with regard to the obligations which the one party has undertaken to the other, such dispute shall be settled by a tribunal of their own constitution. . . .
>
> What is commonly called repudiation or total breach of a contract . . . does not abrogate the contract, though it may relieve the injured party of the duty of further fulfilling the obligation which he has by the contract undertaken to the repudiating party. The contract is not put out of existence though all further performance of the obligations undertaken by each party in favour of the other may cease. It survives for the purpose of measuring the claims arising out of the breach, and the arbitration clause survives for determining the mode of their settlement. The purposes of the contract have failed, but the arbitration clause is not one of the purposes of the contract.[10]

9   [1942] AC 356.
10   Id. at pp. 373-374, 375 and 377.

Regarding alleged termination of the contract on grounds other than repudiation, Simon LC observed that

> where the parties are at one in asserting that they entered into a binding contract, but a difference has arisen between them whether . . . circumstances have arisen which have discharged one or both parties from further performance, such differences should be regarded as differences which have arisen 'in respect of' or 'with regard to', or 'under' the contract, and an arbitration clause which uses these, or similar, expressions should be construed accordingly . . . I do not agree that an arbitration clause expressed in such terms . . . ceases to have any possible application merely because the contract has 'come to an end', as, for example, by frustration. In such cases it is the performance of the contract that has come to an end.[11]

Accordingly, where it is being claimed that the contract has come to an end by virtue of, for example, misrepresentation or non-disclosure, fundamental breach, frustration or the triggering of termination provisions, the arbitrator can deal with these matters, provided the clause is sufficiently wide to embrace such questions.

Facts founding jurisdiction   As is the case with the initial existence of the contract, arbitrators have no power to make a binding decision about the existence of facts which are claimed to found their jurisdiction. Thus, where the arbitration clause in a building contract stipulated that no arbitration shall take place until the construction works had been completed, it was held that the arbitrator had no authority to decide whether or not those works actually were completed.[12] Any decision the arbitrator purported to make on this point did not bind the parties.

In the same vein, where the arbitrator's jurisdiction depends on whether certain notices have been given, generally he has no authority to decide this question.[13]

Illegality   Where it is claimed that the contract, under which the arbitrator is supposed to get his jurisdiction, is illegal *ab initio*, the initial existence of the contract is in dispute and may lie outside the tribunal's authority to determine. On the other hand, where it is claimed that, some time after its conclusion, the contact or its performance became illegal, there is no reason in principle, why this cannot be determined by an arbitrator.

11   Id. at pp. 366-367.
12   *Smith v. Martin* [1925] 1 KB 745.
13   [1942] AC 356.

If it is being contended that the contract is illegal from the very outset, the courts now distinguish between an illegality which would impeach the arbitration clause itself and other kinds of illegality. For instance, it may be claimed that the entire contract, including the arbitration clause, was procured by fraud. By contrast, it may be argued that performance of the contract would be contrary to some common law principle or statutory rule. In *Harbour Assurance Co. v. Kausa General Ltd*[14] the 'orthodox view' that arbitrators can never deal with questions of the underlying contract being void *ab initio* was rejected, principally because the law in this area should strive to give effect to the parties' intentions and their manifest preference for one-stop adjudication. If the parties clearly want the arbitrator to rule on any allegations of invalidity, he should be permitted to do so. Perhaps there may be some forms of invalidity which, for reasons of public policy, fall outside an arbitrator's competence. Leaving these aside, the arbitration clause has an entirely separate legal existence from the main contract; if that contract happens to be illegal in one way or another, it does not follow that the arbitration clause is unlawful and should not be enforced. There is no general public policy objection to arbitrators deciding on questions of illegality, especially when the entire process is subject to a degree of judicial review. On the other hand, present day public policy is strongly in favour of arbitration and extra-curial disputes-resolution, where the parties opt for that method of redressing their grievance.

The position is different where the alleged illegality, if established, would render the arbitration clause itself an entire nullity. And as Hoffman LJ observed in *Harbour Assurance*, '[w]hen one comes to voidness for illegality, it is particularly necessary to have regard to the purpose and policy of the rule which invalidates the contract and to ask . . . whether the rule strikes down the arbitration clause as well. There may be cases in which the policy of the rule is such that it would be liable to be defeated by allowing the issue to be determined by a tribunal chosen by the parties. This may be especially true of *contrats d'adhésion* in which the arbitrator is in practice the choice of the dominant party.'[15]

In *Church & General Insurance Co. v. Connolly*,[16] the question of illegality did not arise until after the award had been made. This was an action to enforce the award and the defence was that public policy prevented its enforcement because the insurance contract, the basis for the award, was illegal. Costello J. held that if the illegality point had been raised during the course of the reference, the arbitrator would have had the jurisdiction to

14   [1993] QB 701.
15   Id. at p.724.
16   Costello J 7 May 1981.

adjudicate on it. And it would not constitute misconduct if he rejected the respondent's contention on this point. But if the court was of the view that there was substance to the illegality claim, it could remit the matter back to the arbitrator for his ruling on the question. In the event, it was held by the court there that the contract was not in breach of the relevant insurance regulations.

Arbitrator's own powers   A difference exists between a dispute about an arbitrator's powers, within his jurisdiction, and about his very jurisdiction to conduct the reference. Assuming the clause in question is sufficiently wide to cover the matter, arbitrators can make effective rulings about what powers they possess; for instance, whether they can direct specific performance or grant a mandatory injunction. Since, however, the question of their powers is a matter of procedural law, rulings on this issue are readily reviewable by the courts.

Scope of the submission   A dispute may very well fall within the terms of an arbitration clause but the dispute actually referred to the arbitrator may not fit that description. It would seem that, if the powers conferred are sufficiently wide, arbitrators are legally competent to make binding decisions about the scope of what was submitted for their determination. Again a decision of this nature is readily reviewable by the courts.

Fraud   There is no reason in principle why arbitrators cannot decide claims of fraud, again if the clause is sufficiently wide to encompass fraud. In such cases, however, s. 39 of the 1954 Act empowers the court to intervene and stop the reference in several ways.[17]

Rectification of contracts   In the *Ashville Investment Ltd* case,[18] it was held that there was no reason in principle why arbitrators cannot direct that the terms of a contract shall be rectified, again assuming the arbitration clause is sufficiently wide to cover the point and rectification is warranted in all the circumstances. Several cases that suggested that there could be no jurisdiction to direct rectification were distinguished as being based on interpretations of the arbitration clauses under consideration in those cases.

Claims in tort   If the arbitration clause is sufficiently wide, the tribunal can deal with claims in tort as well as purely contractual disputes.[19] Usually,

---

17   See post pp. 108-110.
18   [1989] QB 488.
19   E.g. *Aggeliki Charis Co. Maritima S.A. v. Pagnon Spa* [1994] 1 LlLR 169.

claims for damages for negligence can be founded on the parties' contract as well as arising extra-contractually.

DISPUTES AND DIFFERENCES

Even though some issue may fit within the terms of an arbitration clause, usually it cannot be the subject matter of an arbitration unless a dispute or difference regarding the matter has arisen between the parties to the contract. Some clauses go further and require the making of a formal claim before the matter can go to arbitration. Where the clause requires merely a 'dispute or difference', it is a question of fact whether there are such differences between the parties. There must be some form of assertion by one party and a denial or rebuttal by the other.

Occasionally, it can be in the wider interests of a party to resist a claim being made, under an arbitration clause, even though his defence has little or no prospect of success. Where the respondant simply does not believe what he is saying, then there is no real dispute or difference and he would not be entitled, under s. 5 of the 1980 Act,[20] to stay parallel litigation. But it is very difficult to prove that a defence entered is not genuine, albeit misguided.

Where a defence is entered which seems to be entirely unstateable, the requisite dispute exists and the arbitrator can deal with the matter. In such cases, however, the claimant may apply to the court for summary judgment, which almost always will be met by the defendant seeking a stay. The practice in England appears to be for the court to hear both applications together and, if its is satisfied that the defence is a hopeless one, give judgment for the plaintiff.[21] But the power to stay parallel proceedings in England is in the court's discretion, whereas under s. 5 of the 1980 Act there is an absolute entitlement to a stay. It remains to be seem whether a different practice will be followed in Ireland the light of this difference.

AD HOC SUBMISSIONS

An *ad hoc* submission is where the parties agree that a present existing dispute shall be resolved by arbitration. The same general principles regarding agreements to arbitrate future disputes apply to these agreements, regarding their existence, scope and effects. *Ad hoc* submissions frequently

20   See ch. 2.
21   Cf. *Nova (Jersey) Knit Ltd v. Kanngarn Spinners GmbH* [1977] 1 WLR 1713.

contain both an agreement to arbitrate and also the nomination of the arbitrator and a time-table for the pre-hearing procedures. *Ad hoc* submissions are often made where a dispute between the parties is already being arbitrated but a particular matter or matters is not covered by the existing agreement; in such cases, the parties may agree to extend the arbitrator's jurisdiction.

In *Royal Commissioner of Wheat Supplies v. Usher & Co. Ltd*,[22] it was held that an agreement between the parties to a dispute, which was being determined by a statutory arbitrator, that he should determine an incidental question which was not within his statutory jurisdiction, was a valid arbitration agreement. The arbitrator there was appointed to determine the amount of compensation payable for wheat expropriated under war-time regulations. Since the relevant regulations did not empower him to decide who should bear the costs of the reference, the parties agreed that he should determine that matter. The court could 'not see any legal objection to the parties arriving at such a submission, and giving to the statutory arbitrator a power, by consent, to deal with other matters not covered by the statutory arbitration'.[23]

THIRD PARTIES

As a general rule, it is only the parties to the arbitration agreement who acquire rights and incur liabilities under it. There are, however, two qualifications to this principle.

Acquiring rights and duties Section 5 of the 1980 Act provides that a stay granted against parallel litigation applies to 'any person claiming through or under' a party.[24] And s. 27 of the 1954 Act states that an award shall be final and binding on 'the persons claiming under' a party. For instance, if an agreement was made in trust for someone or on his account, for most purposes he is in effect a party to that agreement even though someone else happens to be designated the contracting party. Also, by virtue of the operation of law, one person may succeed to the rights and duties of another; for instance a party's personal representative or where one statutory body succeeds to the rights and liabilities of another. Also too, a person may be subrogated for the rights of another under the general principles of subrogation. And under general principles of contract law, the parties can

22   [1920] 2 IR 483.
23   Id. at p. 487.
24   See ante pp. 25-27.

agree that a new party shall replace one of the original parties, that is, a contract of novation.

Claimant an assignee   Except where there has been novation, duties under a contract cannot be transferred to another (except of course by statute). But rights under most kinds of contract can be assigned; with some contracts, for instance shares in companies and debts owing to registered companies, for there to be an absolute legal assignment certain formalities must be followed. Authority on contractual assignments of arbitration agreements is scanty but the position would appear to be as follows. Assuming that the underlying contract in question is capable of being assigned, the presence in it of an arbitration clause will not prevent its assignment. Where there has been a legal assignment, that is, where it is in writing and the other party to the agreement has been duly notified, the assignee may maintain an arbitration in his own name. If there has been only an equitable assignment, the assignor must join in the arbitration.

Indemnity from third party   Where a claim is being made against X, it often happens that, if X were to be found liable, he in turn would have a good claim for an indemnity against Y; and at times Y in turn may have an indemnity claim against Z, and so on. If a claim is brought against X in the courts then, under the third party procedure provided for in the court rules (for example, Rules of the Superior Courts, O. 16), X can compel Y to come in and defend himself in the same proceedings; Y in turn can do the same to Z, and so on. Where the facts underlying these various disputes are substantially similar there are several advantages in having the entire matter dealt with in the one set of proceedings. It can be far more economical; a party does not have to fight the same issue several times. It avoids the risk of separate proceedings giving rise to contradictory resolution of the same matters.

   One of the main weaknesses in the entire arbitration system is that there is no way in which third parties, against whom a respondent would have a right of indemnity, can be compelled to have that matter adjudicated in the primary arbitration. Even if Y and Z, in the above example, have their own arbitration arrangements with X and with each other, those arrangement may not authorise the arbitrator in the claim against X to deal with the indemnity claims in the same reference. Y and Z may have agreed to arbitrate all of their disputes with X, but that cannot affect arbitration of disputes some other person has with X. Respondents like X here can be in an unenviable position. Often it will not be in the other parties' interests to assist in devising a convenient procedure.

It is common in building contracts and in leases to insert in the arbitration clauses provisions to ensure that certain third-party claims can be dealt with in the same arbitration. Those third parties would often be sub-contractors or sub-lessees.

4

THE ARBITRAL TRIBUNAL

Although for some purposes an arbitration will be regarded as having commenced even though no arbitrator has yet been appointed, it is best to consider his appointment, status, remuneration and the like before addressing the commencement and conduct of the reference.

APPOINTING THE ARBITRATOR

It is a distinctive feature of arbitration that the decision-maker is appointed by the very parties to the dispute. That appointment may be directly by them or indirectly, by authorising some third party to make the nomination. Sometimes the agreement will require that several arbitrators be appointed. If it is silent on the matter, the agreement is deemed to be for reference to a sole arbitrator.[1]

The usual procedure followed for constituting the arbitral tribunal is that the parties exchange the names of several likely arbitrators, or their chosen nominating authority draws up a list of such names. Those persons are then approached informally to see if they are prepared to accept the office. A person who has agreed in principle to act will then be appointed. Formerly, a party to a dispute could easily frustrate an arbitration by merely declining to make an appointment in circumstances where both parties' agreement was required. But the 1954 Act contains several provisions for making appointments in default of agreement or where the nominating authority does not act.

Qualifications The law does not lay down any qualifications for acting as an arbitrator. Any person chosen by both or one of the parties or by the nominating authority, as the case may be, is qualified to act. However, many countries have arbitration associations that train arbitrators and arbitrators often happen to be members of those bodies, such as the London-based

1   1954 Act, s. 14.

Chartered Institute of Arbitrators, which has a world wide membership, including an active branch in Ireland. At times, the agreement between the parties will stipulate qualifications for the arbitrator; in that event only persons so qualified can be appointed. A person with any financial interest in the subject matter of the dispute should disclose the fact to both parties and obtain their assent before agreeing to act.

Sole arbitrator   Usually the arbitral tribunal is comprised of a single person. Unless several arbitrators are expressly provided for, s. 14 of the 1954 Act requires the agreement to be construed as envisaging one person only. An intention to have more than one arbitrator must be stated in the arbitration agreement or in a document to which it refers.

Appointment by agreement   Where the arbitration agreement does not set out any method for constituting the tribunal then the parties must reach agreement about who they will appoint; failing agreement, the court may make the appointment.[2] There is no set formality for an agreement of this kind. But writing or written confirmation is advisable. It also is advisable for the person selected, at the earliest possible stage, to satisfy himself that he was validly appointed, that is, that any procedures or qualifications stipulated in the arbitration agreement have been complied with.

Appointment by third party   Often the arbitration agreement will provide for a third party making the appointment, for instance the president or chairman of a designated professional association. If that person refuses or neglects to make the appointment, there is no statutory provision for dealing with the situation.[3] It has been held that s. 18(a) of the 1954 Act does not apply in those circumstances.[4] Nor, would it seem, is there any mechanism whereby, when an arbitrator appointed by a third party refuses to act or is incapable of acting or dies, the Court can fill the vacancy. In such circumstances, the best course perhaps is to invite the nominating authority to make a fresh appointment. Arbitration agreements often expressly provide a mechanism for resolving this predicament.

Appointment by the court   There are several circumstances where the sole-member tribunal can be constituted by the court under s. 18 of the 1954 Act.

2   Id. s. 18(a).
3   Contrast s. 6(4) of the English Arbitration Act, 1979.
4   *National Enterprises Ltd v. Racal Communications Ltd* [1975] Ch 397.

—*Default of agreement* To take first where there is to be a single arbitrator, whose appointment requires the consent of the parties. If, after 'differences have arisen', the parties to the dispute do not concur in the appointment proposed or made by one of the parties, s. 18(a) authorises that person to serve a written notice on the other or the others requiring them to agree to that person's appointee. If, within seven 'clear days', agreement is not reached and nobody is duly appointed, the person who served the written notice can then apply to the court for it to fill the office. The court's power here is entirely discretionary, although in the absence of special circumstances it probably would lean in favour of granting the application. Whoever the court may appoint then has authority to act in the reference and to make an effective award.

—*Filling a vacancy* Section 18(b) applies the same procedure where an arbitrator who has been appointed refuses to act or is not capable of acting or dies—except in the very unusual case where the terms of the agreement preclude filling such vacancy or provide another method of filling a vacancy.

—*Following revocation or removal* As is explained below,[5] circumstances can arise which justify the court removing an arbitrator from his office or revoking his authority. In such cases, s. 40(2)(i) of the 1954 Act gives the court a discretion to fill the vacancy.

Two arbitrators   Exceptionally the parties will have stipulated for two arbitrators. In such cases, the normal practice is for the two to take up the reference but, if they disagree, they will appoint what is called an umpire to decide the matter. A reference to two arbitrators never involves a three-person tribunal, except of course where the agreement expressly so provides. Instead, the tribunal is the two persons and, where they cannot agree, it becomes a one person (the umpire) tribunal.

Appointment by the parties   Normally each of the parties will appoint his own arbitrator. The procedure to be followed is[6] the other side must be informed of who the party has chosen; the appointee must also be informed; he should be willing to act and indicate his willingness to accept the appointment. He is not appointed until he has accepted the nomination. But he has no power to deal with the reference until his co-arbitrator has been

---

5   Infra p. 54.
6   *Tradex Export S.A. v. Volkswagenwerk AG* [1970] 1 QB 537, at p. 544.

appointed—except where there is a default in the second appointment, thereby constituting him the sole arbitrator.

Vacancy filled by a party   Where one party has not chosen his arbitrator then, unless the agreement provides otherwise, s. 15(2) of the 1954 Act authorises the other party to designate his own appointee as the sole arbitrator, with full powers to make a binding award. Where either of the appointees refuse to act or are incapable of acting or die, again unless the agreement provides otherwise, s. 15(1) of the 1954 Act empowers the party who appointed him to designate someone to act in his place. Such an appointment, however, may be set aside by the court.

Appointment by third party   In two-person arbitrations it is unusual to provide for a third party to make the appointment. At times, however, a third party is given that power in default of an appointment by a party.

Appointment by the court   Section 18(b) of the 1954 Act, discussed above, authorises the court to fill vacancies where any arbitrator refuses to act or is incapable of acting or dies. Where all the arbitrators or the umpire are removed by the court, s. 40(2)(i) of the 1954 Act gives it a discretion to appoint a sole arbitrator in their place. There is no similar power where their authority is revoked by leave of the court.

Three arbitrators   Because of the provision in s. 17 of the 1954 Act, three-member tribunals are unusual in this country—as they were in Britain until a similar section was amended there in 1979.[7] Section 17 deals with where the agreement envisages each party appointing an arbitrator and they, in turn, are to appoint the third arbitrator. In such a case, the agreement is deemed to be for a two person tribunal, the third member constituting an umpire. There are no other statutory provisions dealing with three-member tribunals as such.

An umpire   As has been explained, where there are two arbitrators and they disagree, they often select an umpire to decide the matter; so too under s. 17 of the 1954 Act in the type of three-person tribunal dealt with there. It is most unusual for persons other than the two arbitrators to be authorised to appoint the umpire. Where the two arbitrators disagree, s. 16(2) of the 1954 Act requires them promptly to appoint an umpire. At any time during the reference, either party may apply to the court to order that the umpire shall act as the sole arbitrator.

7   Arbitration Act, 1979, s. 6(2).

REMUNERATION AND EXPENSES

The main extra cost in arbitration, which does not exist in litigation, is the arbitrator's fees and expenses; litigants do not have to pay the judge's salary.

Entitlement Often the parties will have agreed in advance to pay the arbitrator's fee and expenses and what the amount of the fee should be or how it should be calculated. At times an agreement on this issue may not be concluded until after the appointment has been accepted. If payment is not made accordingly, once the award is published the arbitrator is entitled to bring an action to recover the sum due.

Except where it is otherwise agreed, the parties are jointly liable for the tribunal's fees and expenses. That entitlement exists as soon as the reference is complete and an award is made. Whether there is a similar entitlement when the reference concluded at some earlier stage remains a matter for debate.

It is permissible for one party to agree with the arbitrator to pay his remuneration and expenses, so long as the other party is fully aware of that arrangement. But once he accepts the appointment, he may not unilaterally deal with one party in relation to payment of any fee.[8]

Quantum How much the arbitrator is to be paid is a matter to be determined between him and those making the appointment. There is no set scale of fees for arbitrators; the more eminent ones can command substantial fees. Much will depend on matters such as the complexity of the dispute, the novelty of the issues to be decided, the degree of expertise being required, the value of the property or the sum in issue, its importance to the parties, the location of the tribunal, the duration of the reference etc. Often it will not be practicable to estimate at the outset what the actual fee will be but it is advisable that the parties are appraised of the methods which will be used to calculate fees and, preferably, obtain their consent.

Where, for one reason or another, a fixed sum is not appropriate, the following are the principal basis for calculating fees—

i. A percentage of the amount at issue between the parties;

ii. A percentage of the mid-point between the amounts being claimed by both parties;

iii. A rate per day, or per week or per hour; this rate may differ depending on whether the tribunal is sitting or is not actually at hearing.

8   See infra p. 47.

A combination of some of these may be chosen.

Where the quantum has not been agreed, the arbitrator is entitled to be paid a reasonable amount, which will depend on all the circumstances of the reference. If there has been no agreement at all, it would seem that under the principles of *quantum meruit* he is entitled to be paid a reasonable fee. An umpire also would seem to have an implied right to reasonable remuneration, at least where the two arbitrators have agreed and he then takes up the reference. Whether there is any inherent right to payment for his involvement prior to then is a matter that could be debated.

Commitment fee   At times arbitrators will be unsure of when the reference will actually begin, how long it will last and what adjournments or postponements may be sought by the parties. If they agree to accept the appointment, they then are obliged to be available to hear the dispute and often they must reject other work being offered to them during the anticipated duration of the reference. It is for this reason that at times arbitrators look for what is called a commitment fee—payment for simply making time available to deal with the reference, even though the matter may not be at hearing during all or part of that time. It has been held, however, that an arbitrator should not, after accepting the appointment, unilaterally seek a commitment fee from one of the parties.[9] To do so may amount to technical misconduct because at least it gives the appearance of possible bias on his part. Moreover it was suggested there that the question of any commitment fee should be agreed before the arbitrator accepts his appointment.

Taxation of costs   In litigation, where the amount of lawyers' costs and remuneration is being challenged, the matter is resolved by the procedure known as taxation, either by the Taxing Master in the High Court or the County Registrar in Circuit Court actions.[10] In arbitrations the tribunal's fees are regarded as part of the costs and can be measured, in the same way as legal fees, by taxation. The position in this regard under the 1954 Act is slightly different from that in Britain.[11] Provided the parties gave their consent, s. 29(1) of the 1954 Act permits an arbitrator to tax the costs of the reference, including his own fees. Where he does not tax them, they can be taxed by the Taxing Master in the same way and under the same principles as if the award was a judgment of the High Court.

9   *K/S Norjari A/S v. Hyundai Heavy Industries Co.* [1992] QB 863.
10   See generally, D. Casson & I. Dennis eds., *Odgers' Principles of Pleading and Practice* (22nd ed. 1981) pp. 372-375.
11   Their prior consent to taxation by the arbitrator is not required, although arbitrators there are not obliged to carry out the taxation.

Where the parties consented to the arbitrator taxing the costs and then one of them contends that they were taxed at an excessive amount, he cannot then submit the matter to the Taxing Master. His only remedy (apart from refusing to pay) would seem to be attack the award, on the grounds that the arbitrator committed misconduct, for instance by putting his own interests before the parties or carrying out the taxation in an erroneous manner. Clear evidence of misconduct is required; it does not suffice simply to show that the Taxing Master would have determined a lower sum. Where the court finds there was a miscalculation or other error, usually it will remit the matter to the arbitrator to reconsider his taxation.[12] If there was very serious misconduct, the court might even set aside the entire award.[13]

Securing payment   Unless he secures payment in one way or another, the arbitrator may be forced to resort to litigation to recover his fees. Often persons will insist on the fees being secured, either by way of a payment on account or a bank guarantee or a deposit with a stake-holder, before agreeing to commence the reference. If the arbitrator insists on his fees being paid before handing over the award, a party can pay the amount demanded into court, pending taxation, and is then entitled to get the award. Of course if the party who is required to pay the fees accepts the amount charged, he will not seek taxation.

Demanding security   Where the reference has got under way to any significant extent, it may be misconduct on the arbitrator's part for him to start demanding security for his fees at that stage.[14] This is something he should have anticipated at the very beginning. All will depend on the circumstances of the case; if the reference is not very far advanced and now looks as if it will last longer than was anticipated, it is possible that he is justified in calling for security on threat of not continuing any further with the reference. There are no judicial guidelines on what is permitted. However, if he must pay any out of pocket expenses, it would seem that he can insist on security for them at any time.

Lien   Arbitrators are entitled to exercise a lien over their award, meaning they can refuse to hand over the award until they are paid what is due to them. Where a party believes what is being charged is excessive, s. 33 of the 1954 Act enables him to pay into the court the sum being sought, pending

---

12   E.g. *King v. Thomas McKenna Ltd* [1991] 2 QB 480; post p. 126.
13   Cf. the *Norjari* case, supra n.9.
14   Ibid.

taxation, and he then is entitled to be given the award. Perhaps the main weakness with this lien is where the respondent is confident that the award will be in his favour. In that case, he will have no need for the award, since all it will say is that he does not have to pay any money. Nor is there any great incentive for the claimant to take up the award, since it probably will have rejected his claim.

RIGHTS AND DUTIES

An arbitrator's only right in a reference is to be paid his agreed or a reasonable remuneration and expenses. The 1954 Act gives him several powers for conducting the reference, some of which can only be exercised on the direction of the court. Frequently, the arbitration agreement or the terms of the appointment will set out various powers which parties confer on the tribunal. These powers are considered below in dealing with the beginning and the conduct of the reference.

An arbitrator's principal duties are to proceed with reasonable dispatch, to exercise reasonable care and to act impartially. The principal sanctions for breach of these duties are to revoke the arbitrator's authority and to have the award set aside. Arbitrators ordinarily cannot be held liable for negligence; whether that immunity extends to breach of their duty of impartiality is an open question. A possible mode of redress available to an aggrieved party is not to pay the fees and to plead breach of the arbitrator's duties as a defence to an action for the fees.

Impartiality The general principle *nemo iudex in sua causa* applies to arbitrators; they must not be bribed nor allow themselves to be in a position where there is a significant danger that they may show bias.

Apparent bias Justice must not only be done but must be seen to be done. Thus, if the arbitrator has a relationship with one of the parties such that he could very well be likely to decide for or against one of them, he is in breach of his duty. The test, is whether a reasonable person would regard the relationship as too close as to be objectionable: As Blayney J put it in *Bord na Mona v. Sisk & Son Ltd*, would 'a right minded person with full knowledge of the facts have been led to conclude that there was a real likelihood of bias.'[15] There the arbitrator, an architect, had provided professional services to the respondent's (a property developer) associate building

15   Blayney J, 31 May 1990, at p. 12.

company. It was held that, in all the circumstances, there was no real likelihood of bias. If the arbitrator has a share-holding in one of the parties, he should disclose that fact, even where the holding is highly unlikely to affect his decision in any way.[16] Impartiality is also jeopardised where the arbitrator is connected with the subject matter of the reference in such a way as he is likely to lose or gain from the outcome.

Beyond these generalisations, it not really possible to lay down exact rules about what arrangements or relationships would be regarded by the court as antecedent bias. Some assistance can be derived from the many administrative law cases on the *nemo iudex* principle.[17]

Bias in conduct of the reference   During the course of the reference, the arbitrator must strive to show impartiality, especially not to have undue contact with one of the parties. For instance, in *Re Briens' Arbitration*,[18] two arbitrators were appointed to value land, which the parties had worked in partnership, and to determine which of them should have the first offer to purchase it. Under the procedure agreed, each arbitrator was to make a separate valuation of the farm 'on behalf of the party' whom he represented. One of the arbitrators viewed the farm accompanied by the party who had appointed him but not by the other party. It was held that the arbitrator's action was 'contrary to all principles of justice and fair play' and amounted to misconduct. According to Boyd J, the governing principle is that

> When once they enter on an arbitration, arbitrators must not be guilty of any act which can possibly be construed as indicative of partiality or unfairness. It is not a question of the effect which misconduct on their part had in fact upon the result of their proceedings, but of what effect it might possibly have produced. It is not enough to show that, even if there was misconduct on their part, the award was unaffected by it, and was in reality just. . . .[19]

In a more recent instance, *State (Hegarty) v. Winters*,[20] where the arbitrator visited the property which was the subject of the reference accompanied by an employee of one of the parties, it was held that such action might 'reasonably give rise in the mind of an unprejudiced onlooker

---

16   *Sellar v. Highland Rly. Co.* (1919) S.C. 19.
17   See generally, G. Hogan & D. Morgan, *Administrative Law in Ireland* (2nd ed. 1991), pp. 420-439.
18   [1910] 2 IR 84.
19   Id. at pp. 89-90.
20   [1956] IR 320.

to the suspicion that justice was not being done.'[21] The award was set aside on the grounds of the arbitrator's misconduct. By contrast in *Childers Heights Housing Ltd. v. Molderings*,[22] the arbitrator expressed a wish to see the disputed site on her own and neither party raised any objection. It was held that her going to view the site on her own was not misconduct.[23]

Redress   Breach of the *nemo iudex* principle or partial conduct in the course of the reference can be sanctioned under the 1954 Act. Antecedent or actual bias can justify the court revoking the arbitrator's appointment[24] or setting aside the award,[25] as well as the arbitrator being denied remuneration and possibly his out of pocket expenses. If the arbitrator is found to have been in collusion with a party or otherwise corrupt, the court can make him liable for the costs of the application. Whether or in what circumstances an arbitrator can be held liable in damages is an issue which remains to be determined.

Generally, where a party is aggrieved because of bias, especially apparent bias, he is required to make known his objection at the earliest opportunity; if he does not do so, he may be regarded as having waived that ground of objection. Section 39(1) of the 1954 Act provides for an exception to this principle—where the objection is that the arbitrator has a relationship with a party or with the subject of the reference and the objecting party was aware or should have been aware of that relationship at the time he entered into the arbitration agreement and, additionally, the arbitrator was named or designated in that agreement.

Proceed diligently   Arbitrators are required to conduct the reference with all reasonable dispatch; the speed with which matters must be dealt with depends on all the circumstances of the case. Section 24 of the 1954 Act authorises the court to remove arbitrators who 'fail to use all reasonable dispatch in entering on and proceeding with the reference and making an award.' An arbitrator who is removed under this power is deprived of entitlement to be remunerated for his services. It seems unlikely that a party can recover damages for loss suffered in consequence of excessive delay by the tribunal.

Duty of care and immunity from liability   Arbitrators must carry out

21   Id. at p. 336.
22   [1987] ILRM 47.
23   Cf. *L. Duggan & Sons v. Winkens* (Carroll J, 31 July 1987).
24   See infra p. 53.
25   See post pp. 118-119.

their function in a careful and responsible manner; failure to do so, depending on the circumstances, may constitute misconduct, enabling the court under ss. 37 and 38 of the 1954 Act to remove the arbitrator or to set aside his award. But it would seem that he cannot be held liable in damages for any loss caused by his negligence.

It has always been accepted that, at common law, arbitrators cannot be held liable for losses arising in consequence of their negligence, although there is no reported authority where an action for damages against an arbitrator was rejected on those grounds. In *Sutcliffe v. Thackrah*,[26] where the defendant, an architect hired to certify work under a building contract, unsuccessfully claimed the immunity on the grounds that he was a 'quasi-arbitrator', Lord Reid accepted that

> an action will not lie against an arbitrator for want of skill or for negligence in making his award. The reason for this may be that the public interest does not make it necessary for the courts to exercise greater powers over arbitrators than those which they possess, such as the power of removing for misconduct or of correcting errors of law which appear on the face of an award.
>
> Furthermore, as a matter of public policy it has been thought to be undesirable to allow an action against an arbitrator (for lack of care or skill) for the reason that his functions are of a judicial nature. . . .
>
> The immunity of arbitrators from liability for negligence must be based on the belief—probably well founded—that without such immunity arbitrators would be harassed by actions which would have very little chance of success. And it may also have been thought that an arbitrator might be influenced by the thought that he was more likely to be sued if his decision went one way than if it went the other way, or that in some way the immunity put him in a more independent position to reach the decision which he thought right.[27]

When the question was considered again in *Arenson v. Arenson*,[28] a case where an accountant hired to value shares in a company was sued for negligence, some of the Law Lords suggested that not all arbitrators enjoyed immunity from suit. It was suggested that the very fact of being appointed as arbitrator and being subject to the Arbitration Acts does not guarantee immunity where the tribunal's function is 'purely investigatory', and performs 'no function even remotely resembling the judicial function save that

26   [1974] AC 727.
27   Id. at pp. 744 and 736.
28   [1977] AC 405.

he finally decides a dispute or difference with has arisen between the parties.'[29]

Whether or to what extent arbitrators should be afforded immunity is one of public policy. Although arbitrators are seen in the same light as judges, there are significant differences between them, most notable perhaps that, as a condition of appointment, the arbitrator can stipulate that he will not be held liable in negligence. Also, judges' immunity can be based on the Constitution, as an aspect of the guarantee of judicial independence. When the matter comes for consideration in an Irish court, such immunity as may exist at common law will have to be squared with *Byrne v. Ireland*,[30] where the Supreme Court held that claims to immunity from liability at common law require very convincing justification before they will be accepted. Accordingly, it no longer can be taken as axiomatic that an arbitrator appointed under the Arbitration Acts cannot be held liable for losses resulting from performing his functions in a negligent manner. Recent case law on the question of negligence resulting in exclusively financial loss suggests that persons exercising an adjudicative function will not be held liable for reasons of public policy.[31] The model rules of the Irish branch of the Chartered Institute of Arbitrators purport to exclude all liability in negligence.

TERMINATION OF APPOINTMENT

Once an arbitrator publishes his award, his office comes to an end and he is *functus officio* as regards the reference. Arbitrators may resign, although they may incur liability to the parties for resigning in breach of contract. Their authority may be revoked and they may even be removed by the court.

Revoking authority Because at common law a party could revoke the authority of an arbitrator he had appointed, that party could frustrate the entire process by withdrawing the authority. It was to remedy this abuse that s. 9 of the 1954 Act was enacted, which renders the arbitrator's authority irrevocable without the leave of the court. If what the arbitrator is alleged to have done does not amount to misconduct but a party nevertheless wants him removed, an application can be made under this section. The power here does not apply in respect of the arbitrator appointed by the other party,

---

29   Id. at p. 440; see too p. 442.
30   [1972] IR 241.
31   E.g. *Jones v. Dept. of Employment* [1988] 2 WLR 493.

but it would seem to apply where there is a sole arbitrator appointed either by both parties or by an independent nominator. No criteria are laid down to guide the court's discretion in such cases. It has been held that the court should not readily give an applicant leave to revoke an appointment; that the jurisdiction 'ought to be exercised in the most sparing and cautious manner. . . .'[32] Obtaining the court's leave does not automatically result in the arbitrator's removal; it is then for the applicant to make that decision.

Removal   The usual sanction against arbitrators who are unduly dilatory or otherwise negligent, or who display partiality or the appearance of bias, is their removal from the office. Section 24(1) of the 1954 Act empowers the court, on the application of any party to the reference, to remove an arbitrator who 'fails to use all reasonable dispatch' in commencing and proceeding with the reference. An arbitrator who is removed under this power is not entitled to any remuneration that may have accrued to him.[33]

Section 37 of that Act empowers the court to remove an arbitrator who has misconducted himself or the proceedings. Misconduct here is not confined to action which is objectionable in a moral sense, such as acting utterly recklessly or with patent bias or flagrant disregard for fundamental principles of justice. The term means doing something seriously wrong in the course of the reference, such as departing from the agreed procedure for conducting the reference, not adequately hearing both sides. It will depend on the entire circumstances of each case whether there was misconduct for these purposes. But it is not misconduct to make an error of fact or of law in the award.[34] Having undue contact with one of the parties is almost invariably misconduct.[35]

---

32   *Den of Airlie S.S. Co. v. Mitsui & Co.* (1912) 106 LT 451, at p. 454.
33   S. 24(2).
34   *Moran v. Lloyds* [1983] QB 542.
35   Supra pp. 50-51.

5

COMMENCING THE REFERENCE

Before an arbitration can commence, a dispute must have arisen between the parties. What happens next will depend on the terms of their arbitration agreement. For instance, the parties may have agreed that the matter should first be the subject of negotiations or that a mediator should be called in before the dispute can proceed to adjudication. The formal commencement of the reference is when notice is sent calling for the appointment of an arbitrator. Such notice may be to the other party, requesting that he concurs in an appointment or that he appoints someone, or it may be to the appointing authority empowered under the agreement.

The general principles regarding appointing the arbitral tribunal have already been discussed. Before accepting the position, an arbitrator-designate may very well want to negotiate his remuneration and obtain security for its payment. He also may want agreement as to a timetable and to specific powers he may wish to use. Either before or immediately following acceptance, he will consider whether in the circumstances the appointment is a valid one. This will require considering the arbitration agreement and perhaps certain facts in the dispute. Subject to two principal exceptions, an arbitrator is entitled to decide whether he has jurisdiction to proceed with the reference.

If his jurisdiction or authority is challenged on the grounds that there never was an enforceable agreement for an arbitration, this is not a matter on which he is competent to rule.[1] In contrast, and in the absence of provision to the contrary in the agreement, he can make a valid ruling where it is contended that the contract no longer exists or is not enforceable,[2] such as on the grounds of frustration, repudiation or usually supervening illegality. Similarly, if the arbitrator's jurisdiction is founded on the existence of certain facts, this too is a question which, generally, he is not entitled to rule on.[3] Nor is the arbitrator competent to decide if the reference commenced

1   See ante p. 33.
2   See ante p. 34.

later than the prescribed time.

PROCEDURES TO BE FOLLOWED

What procedures must be followed in litigation are set out principally in the rules applicable to the court in question, for instance, the Rules of the Superior Courts (or 'RSC'). How a reference before an arbitrator will be conducted depends mainly on what procedures the parties agreed to and on the arbitrator's directions. Frequently, the parties will have accepted model procedure rules, such as those adopted by the Irish branch of the Chartered Institute of Arbitrators;[4] at times model rules will be adopted subject to several amendments being made. Or the parties may draw up a set of procedures of their own. Depending on the nature of the dispute and the parties, the procedure adopted can vary from extreme formality, like that for a High Court hearing, to extreme informality.

In the London commodity trade there is a form of arbitration which is referred to as 'look and sniff';[5] the arbitrator simply examines a sample of a commodity and then gives the verdict. Especially for small claims, what is called 'documents only' arbitration is very popular;[6] as the name indicates, the tribunal does not hear any witness but decides the dispute on the basis of the books and papers given to it. Particular kinds of arbitrations follow special procedures and the parties electing for one of those tribunals will be deemed to have chosen their traditional procedures.

Procedures agreed in advance   Often the main features of the procedure which the tribunal is to follow will be agreed by the parties prior to the reference commencing. For instance, they may have agreed to follow one of the many model set of rules or they may have agreed to an approach which is customary in a particular trade or activity. If the reference is to be conducted in a highly formal manner, arrangements will be made for matters such as the exchange of pleadings, discovery and inspection of documents, what evidence may be given and the like. Alternatively, a relatively informal approach may have been agreed on. Certain procedural arrangements may be the subject of implied agreement; or express terms of what was agreed may suggest tacit agreement on other procedural steps, as also may the subject matter of the underlying contract, the nature of the dispute and the

3   See ante p. 35.
4   Reproduced post p. 149.
5   Described in R. Bernstein, *Handbook of Arbitration Practice* (2nd ed. 1993) part 4.
6   Described in id. part 5.

identity of the tribunal. Often arbitrators will insist on certain procedural requirements as a condition of accepting the appointment; for instance, they may demand a very extensive procedural authority to deal with any problem in such manner as they see fit.

Whatever procedure is agreed in advance, the arbitrator is bound to follow it; adherence to that procedure is one of the conditions of his appointment. This, however, is subject to the qualification that the procedure intrinsically must be one of arbitration and not, for instance, be a valuation. Also, a court will disregard certain procedural stipulations that contravene public policy. There is little modern judicial guidance about what the very minimum of procedural propriety requires, which the parties cannot waive by agreement. In the past, agreement to allow in inadmissible evidence and to exclude all legal representation was regarded as profoundly objectionable; it is inconceivable that a court would take the same view today. It is difficult to imagine a genuine procedural short-cut which would be rejected today on grounds of public policy. On the other hand, the powers of supervision which the 1954 Act confers on the High Court most likely would be regarded as peremptory and cannot be contracted out of, except where that Act so allows or in the case of some international arbitrations.[7]

There are also certain coercive powers which, it has been held, can only be exercised by a court and not by a consensual tribunal, such as the power to imprison for contempt of the tribunal.

Procedures agreed after the appointment Many arbitrators prefer not be tied from the outset to some pre-ordained schedule of procedures but instead to devise with the parties the most appropriate procedure for the kind of reference being undertaken. What has been said above concerning what has been impliedly agreed and what procedures are unacceptable on grounds of public policy equally applies in this context. The most important difference is that the tribunal is not strictly bound by a procedure adopted following the appointment. But this does not mean that any agreed procedure can be readily disregarded. At the very least, where it is proposed to deviate from some procedure, which has been agreed on, the tribunal should notify the parties of its intention to do so. If both parties object to what is being proposed, then the originally agreed procedure should be followed.

No agreed procedure Where there has been no agreement at all on the procedure to be followed, the tribunal has a wide discretion to deal with the reference appropriately, provided its approach is intrinsically adversarial

---

7   *CBI (NZ) Ltd v. Badger Chiyoda* [1989] 2 NZLR 669; see post p. 117.

and the tenets of 'natural justice', or of a 'fair trial' are adhered to.

Fair trial   The various procedural rules published by trade associations and by the Chartered Institute are designed to ensure that the issues between the parties are tried fairly. But persons and bodies will differ as to the best precise method of achieving that objective. There are certain procedures and rules that some would regard as an essential feature of a fair hearing but others would attach comparatively little importance to them, such as whether the rules of evidence applicable in the courts should be followed. Persons from an exclusively common law background would tend to place great value on adversary methods whereas civilians might be more amenable to arbitrators acting to a degree as inquisitors, going out themselves and searching for evidence.

The maxims *audi alteram partem* and *nemo iudex in sua causa* sum up the essence of fair procedures and are commonly referred to as the principles or rules of natural justice. *Nemo iudex* has already been considered;[8] the arbitrator must not be unduly partial to one side or hostile to another, nor appear to be partial. *Audi alteram partem* signifies that each side must be afforded equal opportunity to present their case and an award will be set aside where the tribunal departs from this principle. What exactly *audi alteram partem* requires depends very much on the nature of the dispute. Generally, it demands that the parties be given sufficient notice of the time and place for the hearing; that they have adequate opportunity to give evidence and make submissions; that each party be given the chance to contradict the other's case.

There is a host of reported authorities, many of them old, about what constitutes fair procedures in arbitrations. But those cases should be treated with some caution because more recently courts have shown greater tolerance of informality. In the context of London commercial arbitration, McNair J once observed that 'great care has to be used in reading the decisions of a century or half a century ago as to the powers of arbitrators today. . . . The growth of commercial arbitration in the City has been so wide and, as a whole, so beneficial, that the courts show increasing reluctance to interfere with the manner in which these trade bodies carry out their important functions and only interfere in the very rare case where it has been shown that some real impropriety has been committed.'[9]

A matter that has not been thoroughly considered in the courts in recent years is the extent to which arbitrators may resort to inquisitorial-style

---

8   See ante pp. 49-51.
9   *Henry Bath & Sons Ltd v. Birgby Products* [1962] 1 LlLR 389, at p.399.

procedures, without the consent of the parties. For instance, when may the arbitrator rely on his own investigations into the subject matter of the dispute? When, if ever, may the tribunal appoint its own expert to resolve an issue? The conventional view appears to be that common law-style arbitrations envisage an adversary approach. Accordingly, refusal to allow a party cross-examine the other party's witness can be a ground for removing the arbitrator.[10] By contrast, if the arbitrator wants to inspect some location on his own and the parties do not object, there is nothing wrong with the arbitrator going and making that inspection.[11]

THE TRIBUNAL'S POWERS

What powers a court has in the conduct of litigation are set out principally in the rules applicable to the court in question. The powers possessed by an arbitral tribunal are those conferred on it by the agreement of the parties, those given by s.19(1) of the 1954 Act and also, indirectly, certain powers that the High Court can exercise under its rules of procedure. Arbitrators are not obliged to exercise each and every power conferred on them; the powers are at the discretion of the arbitral tribunal to be used when appropriate to enable the tribunal to reach the correct conclusion.

Express powers The principal source of the arbitrator's powers is the parties' agreement; this may or may not set out in detail what he can or cannot do.

For instance, where the Chartered Institute's Irish Branch rules apply, the arbitrator is empowered to:

(1) determine any question as to the validity, extent or continuation in force of any contract between the parties;

(2) order the correction or amendment of any such contract, and of the arbitration agreement, submission or reference, but only to the extent required to rectify any manifest error, mistake or omission which he determines to be common to all the parties;

(3) determine any question of law arising in the arbitration . . .;

(4) determine any question as to his own jurisdiction;

(5) determine any question of good faith, or dishonesty arising in the

---

10   *Chilton v. Saga Holidays* [1986] 1 All ER 841.
11   *Childers Heights Housing Ltd v. Molderings Ltd* [1987] ILRM 47.

dispute;

(6) order any party to furnish him with such further details of its case, in fact or in law, as he may require;

(7) proceed in the arbitration following the failure or refusal of any party to comply with these Rules or with his orders or directions, or to attend any meeting or hearing, but only after giving that party written notice that he intends to do so;

(8) receive and take into account such written or oral evidence as he shall determine to be relevant, whether or not strictly admissible in law;

(9) make one or more interim awards;

(10) order the parties to make interim payments towards the costs of the arbitrator;

(11) hold meetings and hearings in Ireland and elsewhere;

(12) express his award in any currency;

(13) award interest on any sum from and to any date and at such rates as he determines to be appropriate, provided that interest has been claimed or counter-claimed as special damages; or he finds the sum to have been due but not paid up to the date of the award; or he finds the sum to have been paid late but after the commencement of the proceedings;

(14) correct any accidental mistake or omission in his award,

(15) apportion the parties' costs in the arbitration between the parties;

(16) require witnesses to be examined on oath or affirmation and administer oaths to or take affirmation of witnesses;

(17) direct on such terms and conditions as he may determine that evidence be given by affidavit.

Unless the parties at any time agree otherwise, the arbitrator shall have power, on the application of any of party or of his own motion, but in either case only after hearing or receiving any representations from the parties, to:

(1) allow other parties to be joined in the arbitration with their express consent, and make a single final award determining all disputes between them;

(2) allow any party, upon such terms (as to costs and otherwise) as he shall determine, to amend its Statement of Claim, Defence or Reply;

(3) extend or abbreviate any time limits provided by these Rules or by his directions;

(4) rely on his own expert knowledge and experience in any field, provided that the parties have been informed of his being possessed of such knowledge or experience;

(5) appoint one or more advisors or experts on any matter (including law) to assist him in the arbitration;

(6) direct the parties to submit to him, for subsequent exchange, written statements (whether or not verified by oath or affirmation) of the proposed evidence of experts, and direct which of the makers of such statements are to attend before him for oral examination;

(7) order the parties to make any property or thing available for his inspection, and inspect it in the presence of the parties;

(8) order the parties to produce to him, and to each other, and to supply copies of any documents or classes of documents in their possession or power which he determines to be relevant;

(9) order the preservation or storage, of any property or thing under the control of any of the parties and which property or thing is the subject of the reference;

(10) make interim orders for security for any party's own costs, and or to secure all or part of any amounts in dispute in the arbitration.

Implied powers Where the agreement does not state the arbitrator's powers, he has a very wide discretion as to how the entire reference is to be conducted. As Lord Diplock put it, in such cases

> the parties make the arbitrator the master of the procedure to be followed in the arbitration. Apart from a few statutory requirements under the Arbitration Act (1954), . . . he has a complete discretion to determine how the arbitration is to be conducted from the time of his appointment to the time of his award, so long as the procedure he adopts does not offend the rules of natural justice.[12]

This very extensive authority is founded on s. 19(1) of the 1954 Act

12 *Bremer Vulkan case* [1981] AC 909, at p. 985.

which states that, in the absence of a contractual stipulation to the contrary, the arbitrator is entitled to 'do all such other things which during the proceedings on the reference [he] may require.' Thus, arbitrators can order the discovery of documents,[13] the administration of interrogatories[14] and also the inspection of property which is the subject of the dispute,[15] as those procedures assist the tribunal in coming to the correct conclusion.

Section 19 of the 1954 Act gives arbitrators several specific powers, in the absence of any contrary provision in the agreement. They are empowered to examine, on oath or affirmation, any of the parties to the dispute or persons claiming under them. They can direct that witnesses shall be examined on oath or affirmation, and they can administer the oath or affirmation. They can also direct that all documents within the parties' power or possession shall be produced for the hearing.

Because striking out a claim for want of prosecution does not facilitate determination of the dispute, such a power does not fall within s. 19(1).[16] For the same reason, there is no inherent authority to order that two or more arbitrations be consolidated.[17] Where a dispute arises about what powers the arbitrator can exercise, the matter can be referred to the Court for directions under the case stated procedure.[18]

Supplemental powers of the court   Except where they are conferred by the agreement or under s. 19, arbitrators do not possess the following powers but, on application, the court can give directions regarding exercising such powers in connection with the reference. These are enumerated in s. 22 of the 1954 Act, being

(a) security for costs;

(b) discovery and inspection of documents and interrogatories;

(c) the giving evidence by affidavit;

(d) examination on oath of any witness before an officer of the court or any other person, and the issue of a commission or request of the examination of a witness out of the jurisdiction;

(e) the preservation, interim custody or sale of any goods which are the subject matter of the reference;

13   *Kursell v. Timber Operators & Contractors Ltd* [1923] 2 KB 202.
14   Ibid.
15   *Vasso (Owners) v. Vasso (Owners of Cargo)* [1983] 1 WLR 838.
16   *Bremer Vulcan* case [1981] AC 909.
17   *Oxford Shipping Ltd v. Nippon Yusen Kaisha* [1984] 3 All ER 835.
18   See post p. 112.

(f) securing the amount in dispute in the reference;

(g) the detention, preservation or inspection of any property or thing which is the subject of the reference or as to which any question may arise therein, and authorising for any of the purposes aforesaid any persons to enter upon or into any land or building in the possession of any party to the reference, or authorising any samples to be taken or any observation to be made or experiment to be tried which may be necessary or expedient for the purpose of obtaining full information or evidence; and

(h) interim injunctions or appointment of a receiver.

6

PRE-HEARING MATTERS

The pre-hearing stage of the reference is vitally important and it would seem that a considerable number of arbitrations are settled before the hearing opens. Usually, the parties will arrange a preliminary meeting with the arbitrator for a general consideration of the issues and of the procedures to be followed, such as regarding pleadings, discovery of documents, expert witnesses statements. They may also agree on where exactly the hearing shall take place, the time-table and any further pre-hearing meetings. Where the issues are in any way complex, the exchange of pleadings (that is, points of claim, defence, reply) occurs and, often, an exchange of written proofs of evidence. Where the issues are relatively straight-forward, an exchange of statements of facts and contentions may suffice. Applications for security for costs and for interim protection orders may be entertained. Because there is an enormous variety of arbitration procedures, not all the matters set out here may be addressed in a particular reference, nor in the sequence in which they are set out here.

PRELIMINARY MEETING

Where the reference is likely to involve matters of some complexity, a preliminary meeting will take place between the arbitrator and the parties or their representatives. At that stage, account can be taken of the parties' own suggestions about how the reference is to be conducted and potential disagreements can be resolved. The arbitrator will be anxious to obtain a general picture of the issues involved, in order that he can plan the most efficient conduct of the reference. In the more formal kind of proceedings, orders may be made regarding pleadings, discovery and admitting evidence. At times, there may be a subsequent follow up meeting to deal with any additional matters that may have arisen. And in very complex disputes, there may be a very formal pre-trial review just before the hearing gets under way.

The following matters may be dealt with at the preliminary meeting unless they have been clarified by the arbitration agreement:

(1) The arbitrator(s) appointment and remuneration.

(2) Defining the issues, for example, by pleadings; by the exchange of points of claim and points of defence: or by allowing existing documents to stand as pleadings.

(3) Should any other parties be joined; if so is there any provision in the contracts making this possible, and do the parties want to do it?

(4) Discovery; whether appropriate and, if so at what stage and to what extent?

(5) Directions as to the times for taking of the various steps; combine speed in obtaining an award with giving each party a fair opportunity to prepare his case.

(6) Are the arbitrator's existing powers adequate to deal with problems likely to arise; are additional powers required.

(7) Is any major question of law likely to arise? If so should a legal assessor be appointed or should a case be stated to the High Court. If the arbitrator is not a lawyer, should he have power to take legal advice if so minded; and if so, do the parties wish to agree upon the legal adviser to be consulted? And should they be shown the advice when received?

(8) If there is to be a hearing, where is the most convenient place to hold it?

(9) Should all the issues be dealt with at once, or should they be split in some way so that interim awards can be given on some of them.

(10) If expert witnesses are to be called, by what date should their proofs of evidence be exchanged?

(11) Is the arbitrator to be bound by the strict rules of evidence?

(12) If there is to be a hearing, a date should be set by which the parties' representatives are to agree upon, and send to the arbitrator, a list of the issues he has to decide. If they cannot agree upon a list, each should send his own formulation of the issues to be presented.

(13) If there is to be a hearing, a date should be set by which a bundle or bundles of agreed documents are to be sent to the arbitrator so that he may read them, together with the pleadings or their equivalent and the list of issues, before the hearing begins.

(14) Ascertain if the parties wish the aribrator to tax such costs as he may award.

LIMITATION PERIODS

A duly appointed tribunal may not be able to proceed with the reference because the matter is time-barred. The time for proceeding with the reference may be barred by a clause in the contract or by the Statute of Limitations, 1957. An important distinction exists between making a claim and commencing the arbitration. Most statutory limitation provisions focus on actually commencing proceedings. But limitation clauses in arbitration agreements may focus on a party making a formal complaint to the other party rather than on initiating the actual reference.

Statute of limitations The time limits within which proceedings under various heads must be brought are set out principally in the Statute of Limitations, 1957. Thus, actions for breach of a simple contract and for tort must be brought within six years of the cause of the action arising.[1] But the period is three years if the claim is for damages for personal injuries.[2] Claims under the 'Hague Rules' on bills of lading must be brought within one year of the goods being delivered[3] and claims under the 'Warsaw' Convention on the carriage of goods by air have a two years time bar.[4]

Part IV of the 1957 Statute applies its provisions and the provisions of any other legislation on limitations to arbitration.[5] For these purposes, commencing an arbitration is equivalent to bringing an action; it constitutes either serving a written notice requiring the appointment or the concurrence in the appointment of an arbitrator or, where the agreement requires that the dispute be referred to a designated person, referring the matter to him. Generally, the arbitrator has authority to determine whether the dispute is out of time under these enactments. There are no provisions authorising the courts or arbitrators to extend the periods laid down by the Statute of Limitations and comparable legislation. Where the Court sets aside an award or rules that it shall not have effect, the period between arbitration commencing and the Court's order is excluded for the purpose of computing statutory limitation provisions.[6]

Contractual time bars It is quite common for arbitration agreements to stipulate that the claim must be brought or that the arbitration shall be had

1   1957 Act s. 11(1)(a) and (2)(a).
2   Id. s. 11(2)(b).
3   Art. 3(b).
4   Art. 29.
5   1957 Act s. 75; cf. 1954 Act s. 42.
6   1954 Act, s. 44.

within a specified period. Where the Hague Rules apply by virtue of a 'clause paramount' in a bill of lading, rather than by virtue of the Merchant Shipping Act, 1954, the Rules' one year period is a contractual stipulation.[7]

Scope for the time bar   Where what is barred is resort to arbitration, the underlying claim is not affected by the clause and can be brought in the courts. Clauses usually tend to be of the claim-barring type; occasionally they will even specify the manner in which the claim must be stipulated. In England the courts have insisted on particularity in the notice of claim for these purposes: there must be 'such notice as will enable the party to whom it is given to take steps to meet the claim by preparing and obtaining appropriate evidence for that purpose.'[8] But it is not essential to go so far as notifying the other party of the appointment of an arbitrator or requesting the agreed appointing authority to nominate one. Of course, the contract may stipulate for that. For instance, the Hague Rules have been construed to require serving such a notice[9] and the 'Centracon' charterparty has been construed as requiring both a written notice of the claim to be served and that an arbitrator be appointed within three months of the cargo being discharged.[10]

Extension of time   Section 45 of the 1954 Act empowers the court, where imposing the contractual time-bar would cause 'undue hardship' in the circumstances of the case, to direct that the agreed period be extended for such time as it thinks proper. But any extension of time under section 45 must not exceed the relevant statutory limitation period. Sometimes a time limit stipulation in an arbitration clause will give the arbitrator a discretion, like that of the court, to extend that time in an appropriate case. If an arbitrator in such an instance refuses to extend the time, the court still has jurisdiction under s. 45 to consider the application for an extension and must make its own assessment of whether indeed there would be undue hardship caused.[11]

In England the courts used to adopt a somewhat strict stance regarding what amounts to 'undue hardship' until a case in 1967, where it was said that

These time-limit clauses used to operate most unjustly. Claimants used

7   *Nea Agrex SA v. Baltic Shipping Co.* [1976] QB 933.
8   *Rendal A/S v. Arcos Ltd* [1937] 3 All ER 577, at p. 580.
9   Supra n. 7.
10 *Jadranaska Slobodna Plovidba v. Oleagine SA* [1984] 1 WLR 300.
11 *Comdel Commodities Ltd v. Siporex Trade SA (No. 2)* [1991] AC 148.

to find their claims barred when, by some oversight, they were only a day or two late. In order to avoid that injustice, the legislature intervened so as to enable the courts to extend the time. . . . 'Undue' there simply means excessive. It means greater hardship than the circumstances warrant. Even though a claimant has been at fault himself, it is an undue hardship on him if the consequences are out of proportion to his fault.[12]

Regarding what matters should be considered in determining if there will be 'undue hardship', it was said that

the court must take all the relevant circumstances of the case into account, the degree of blameworthiness of the claimants in failing to appoint an arbitrator within the time, the amount at stake, the length of the delay, whether the claimants have been misled, whether through some circumstances beyond their control it was impossible for them to appoint an arbitrator in time. In the last two circumstances . . . normally the power would be exercised. . . . One very important circumstance is whether there is any possibility of the other side having been prejudiced by the delay.[13]

The relevant considerations were spelt out somewhat more systematically as follows:

(1) The words 'undue hardship' . . . should not be construed too narrowly. (2) 'Undue hardship' means excessive hardship and, where the hardship is due to the fault of the claimant, it means hardship the consequences of which are out of proportion to such fault. (3) In deciding whether to extend time or not, the court should look at all the relevant circumstances of the particular case. (4) In particular the following matters should be considered: (a) the length of the delay, (b) the amount at stake, (c) whether the delay was due to the fault of the claimant or to circumstances outside of his control, (d) if it was due to [his] fault, . . . the degree of such fault, (e) whether the claimant was misled by the other party, (f) whether the other party has been prejudiced by the delay and, if so, the degree of such prejudice.[14]

In deciding whether there was indeed undue hardship on the claimant, one

---

12 *Liberia Shipping Corp. 'Pegasus' v. A. King & Sons Ltd* [1967] 2 QB 86 at p. 98.
13 Id. at p. 107.
14 *Comdel* case, supra n. 11, at p. 166. Cf. *Walsh v. Shield Insurance Co.* [1976-7] ILRM 218.

of the matters that may be taken into account is whether he would have a claim against his solicitors in negligence for not being in time.[15]

DEFINING THE ISSUES

Before a dispute can properly be resolved, the issues between the parties should be accurately defined; this will clarify for each party the contentions he has to meet, will assist the tribunal in planning the orderly conduct of the reference and may even assist the parties in settling the matter before any hearing commences. In many types of dispute the issues will be quite clear from the outset. In such cases, a brief discussion of the issues may take place, with a note made of the outcome. If the matter is not entirely straight-forward, the arbitrator may require the parties to set out the bones of their case in brief informal letters. Or the issues may be sufficiently complex to require full written statements of each party's case or High Court-style pleadings.

Written statements of case   This is a document in which a party sets out the main facts of his case in summary form, the propositions of law he will be advancing and an outline of the supporting arguments. Statements of this kind resemble briefs filed in American courts; the arbitration rules of the International Chamber of Commerce (ICC) prescribe in detail what these statements must contain.[16] These enable the tribunal at the outset to form a very clear picture of the nature of the dispute.

Pleadings   Alternatively, the parties may be ordered to exchange pleadings. These are the kind of documents that precede the hearing of most High Court cases but eminent commentators have observed that they are not the ideal way of isolating the central issues in a dispute;[17] often it is not clear from the pleadings what the issues of law will be and there will be little indication of the nature of the evidence. It has been suggested that pleadings should normally be reserved for where the issues are complex, where there is likely to be a full hearing with oral evidence and where the parties will be legally represented.[18]

Further particulars   A party may want the other to elaborate on various

15   *Unitramp SA v. Jenson & Nicholson (S) Pte Ltd* [1992] 1 WLR 862.
16   Art. 13(1).
17   *Mustill & Boyd* at p. 319.
18   Ibid.

points made in his pleadings. To do this he will seek a direction that the other furnish him with further and better particulars of those points.

Notice to admit facts   Where a party is confident that he can establish by evidence certain facts but it will be time-consuming or expensive for him to do so, he may seek a direction that the other side shall admit those facts. If they are not then admitted and are subsequently established at the hearing, then the party who declined to admit them may be required to pay the costs of proving them.

Interrogatories   This procedure is a series of questions delivered to a party, which he must answer on oath either 'yes' or 'no'. While an arbitrator can allow interrogatories to be administered, they are rarely used in arbitrations. An alternative is an open letter to the other party, setting out the various questions. Refusal to answer these may result in a costs penalty.

Amending pleadings   A party may apply to amend his pleadings before the hearing and, indeed, exceptionally during the hearing. The tribunal has a discretion to allow any amendments sought, but may impose some costs sanction where the other party is being thereby inconvenienced. A tribunal will be confronted with an acute dilemma when a substantial amendment is sought almost on the eve of the hearing; to permit a major change at that late stage could pose serious difficulties for the other party and indeed for the conduct of the entire reference. If a proposed amendment will cause a considerable delay, the tribunal will want to ensure that the other party is not unduly prejudiced.

DISCOVERY AND INSPECTION OF DOCUMENTS

In High Court proceedings, before a case goes to trial, a party may obtain an order that the other side shall discover and allow inspection of all relevant documents in his possession or which he can obtain.[19] That other party must then swear an affidavit listing all such documents which may have a bearing on the issues in the case, even documents which he would much prefer not to disclose. This procedure acknowledges the unique value of documentary evidence over oral testimony and is based on the principle that each side in a case should be aware of all documents the other side has relating to the issues in contention.

---

19   See generally, P. Matthews & H. Malek, *Discovery* (1992).

One of the implied powers that arbitrators possess, by virtue of s. 19(1) of the 1954 Act, is to order discovery of documents.[20] It can be a matter of fine judgment how extensive a discovery should be ordered. Ordinarily there will be no discovery until any pleadings have closed.

In one of the leading cases on discovery, it was held that 'every document relates to the matters in question in the action, which not only would be evidence upon any issue, but also which it is reasonable to suppose contains information which *may*—not which *must*—either directly or indirectly enable the party requiring the affidavit either to advance his own case or to damage the case of his adversary.'[21] Unless a party has listed a particular document in his affidavit of discovery, he will not be allowed to tender it in evidence. A party may seek specific as well as general discovery, that is, of identified documents or an identified category of documents. A party must allow inspection by the other party of the documents discovered and copies may be made. Although all relevant documents must be listed, a party can refuse to permit inspection of some of them where they are privileged—notably, communications between the party and his lawyers preparatory to the case in question.

Discovery can be a time-consuming process. At times an enormous amount of material of the most tenuous relevance may be divulged. In the United States, discovery is far more extensive than in Britain and Ireland; by contrast, in Continental Europe discovery as such hardly exists. There also is the question whether a party who is directed to discover documents conscientiously does so; if not, very material information may be withheld from the tribunal and the other side may be unfairly disadvantaged. If a party believes the other has not made full discovery, he may apply for an order for additional discovery, specifying the nature and type of documents he is looking for.

EVIDENCE

It may be necessary to resolve several questions about what evidence the tribunal may be expected to consider.

Rules of evidence   First and foremost is whether the rules of evidence for court proceedings will apply,[22] especially the 'hearsay' rule, which greatly

20   *Kursell v. Timber Operators & Contractors Ltd* [1923] 2 K.B. 202.
21   *Compagnie Finciere etc. du Pacifique v. Peruvian Guiano Co.* (1882) 11 QB 57, at p. 63.
22   See generally, C. Fennell, *The Law of Evidence in Ireland* (1991).

affects what documents can be admitted. Except where the parties otherwise agree, the tribunal is constrained by the ordinary rules of evidence.

Agreeing the documents   Because it is far cheaper to copy every document that may have some bearing on the case and include it in the files to be handed in to the tribunal, than to read every one carefully and pick out only those which will be used, there is a strong tendency to give the tribunal far more documents than are really needed. This tendency was not as marked before widespread use became made of photocopying machines. Formerly, the solicitor and junior counsel would choose only the most essential documents and then have them retyped. Where the tribunal is given a near indiscriminate mountain of paper, considerable delays can be caused and expense incurred. Accordingly, arbitrators sometimes direct the parties to put in only those document they are reasonably confident will be referred to and, additionally, that the files and pagination should be agreed between them. Where that is done, a quick perusal of the statement of case and of the index of documents should enable the tribunal to grasp what the issues are and how the reference is likely to run. Some kinds of arbitrations are determined entirely on the documents submitted and written arguments.[23]

A distinction must be drawn between what documents go in 'as documents' and go in 'as evidence'. In the former case, the parties simply agree that the document in question exists and is authentic. In the latter case, the parties agree that the actual contents of the document are correct. For instance, if a document states that goods were inspected at a particular time and place, the parties accept that this is what the document states and is evidence of the inspection. However, a party is not precluded by such an admission from adducing evidence which denies the veracity of statements in the document.

Written proofs of evidence   Except in cases which are heard on affidavit, a party to litigation will not know what evidence his opponent's witnesses will give, nor will the court have any idea in advance of what kind of evidence to expect. There is a practice in Britain, when evidence is to be given by expert witnesses, that a written summary of the evidence will be provided in advance to the other side. In some Continental European countries, statements containing the evidence to be given by all witnesses must be exchanged before the trial. It is a matter for the arbitral tribunal and the parties whether they should adopt a similar practice, which has much to

---

23   I.e. 'documents-only' arbitrations, described in R. Bernstein, *Handbook of Arbitration Practice* (2nd ed. 1993) parts 3 and 5.

recommend it. Exchanging witness statements reduces the element of surprise in the reference and should encourage settlement.

Listing the issues   In some arbitrations, where the issues are going to be quite complex, the tribunal may direct the preparation of a final list of the issues to be determined. Usually this will not be done until any discovery and inspection of documents has been completed and the hearing is almost ready to begin. Clarifying the issues at a kind of pre-hearing review will help to focus attention on the most contentious issues; it will assist settlement, or at least settlement of several of the less contentious issues; it will facilitate planning the conduct of the reference.

INTERIM PROTECTION ORDERS

Occasionally the safety or very existence of the subject matter of a dispute may be in jeopardy or there is a risk of important evidence being destroyed before the hearing commences. In litigation the High Court has extensive jurisdiction to make the necessary interim orders for protection, for instance an interlocutory injunction preserving the status quo, the so-called *Mareva* injunction, the appointment of a receiver and orders preserving property in dispute and securing the amount in dispute. Except where the arbitration agreement gives authority to do so, the making of an interim protection order does not fall within an arbitrator's usual authority, such as directions that money, the subject of the dispute, should be paid into a bank account or not paid into a bank account, that certain property should be taken into custody or that a receiver be appointed over it. But a party can apply to the court under ss. 22(f)–(g) of the 1954 Act for orders along any of these lines.

SECURITY FOR COSTS

Ordinarily, where the tribunal finds in favour of a defendant or respondent, it will direct that the party who brought the claim should pay the costs of the defence. At times, however, there can be a distinct risk that an order to pay costs will not be complied with; the party may be insolvent or he may not have sufficient assets in the country against which a costs order can be executed. In litigation, in an appropriate case the court will direct a plaintiff to pay a certain amount in advance into court, to ensure that a costs order is met in the event of the defendant eventually succeeding. Unless the arbitration agreement empowers the arbitrator to make such an order, he has no authority to do so.[24] But a party can apply to the court under s. 22(a) of the 1954 Act for an order of that nature.[25]

Whether an order to secure the costs shall be granted is within the court's discretion. Generally, it is disposed to so ordering where it is established that the claimant either is a company which is insolvent or else is a person or body ordinarily resident abroad. Even in these cases the court will take some account of the nature of the arbitration, the complexity of the issues and the strength of the respondent's case. It has been held that applications of this nature are inconsistent with the very scheme and spirit of the rules for ICC arbitrations and should be rejected by the courts in references under those rules.[26] It also has been held that, generally, security for costs should not be ordered where the arbitration is on documents only, merely because the claimant resides abroad.

SETTLEMENT

Ordinarily, offers of settlement will be made before the hearing gets under way; if a party believes the other's offer is not entirely unreasonable, they may enter into negotiations with a view to reaching a settlement. Discussions of that nature are always on a 'without prejudice' basis, meaning whatever took place between the parties during negotiations cannot be disclosed to the arbitral tribunal. It would seem that most arbitrations are settled before the hearing commences and some are even settled during the course of the hearing itself.

As is explained later when discussing the question of costs,[27] there are three principal kinds of offers, viz. the 'open' offer, the offer 'without prejudice' and the offer 'without prejudice except as to costs'. Usually offers will be made on one or other of these two 'without prejudice' basis. At times there may be some strategic advantage in making an 'open' offer; the arbitrator may then see that the offeror is being reasonable and the other party is being unduly intransigent. Once the tribunal knows what a party is offering, that knowledge may influence the tribunal in its ultimate decision on the merits of the claim. Where a party makes an offer of settlement to the other side, generally that is deemed to include an offer to pay all of that side's costs up to the date of the offer. It is preferable, however, to have the

---

24   *Re Union Stearinerie Lanza & Weiner* [1917] 2 KB 558.
25   Cf. *Mavani v. Ralli Bros. Ltd* [1973] 1 WLR 408.
26   *Bank Mellat v. Helliniki Techniki SA* [1984] 1 QB 295.
27   Post pp. 92-93.

question of the entire costs, including the arbitrator's remuneration and expenses, expressly dealt with in the offer. A reasonable time should be allowed for the offeree to consider acceptance of the proffered settlement.

Where a party's offer is accepted then the dispute is settled. Normally that settlement will involve the making of a payment, at times in staged payments at the times and in the sums agreed. A settlement may also require a party to take certain action or to refrain from acting in some manner. Usually the settlement will include provisions regarding who will bear all or part of the costs of the reference.

The settlement may take the form of an agreement between the parties. If it takes that form, it is enforceable in the same way as any other contract between the parties. In order to enhance enforceability, they may seek to have an award made by the tribunal embodying the terms of their settlement. In that way the settlement is enforceable as a arbitral award.[28] However, because arbitrators generally become *functus officio* once the parties have settled their differences, if they want their compromise to take the form of an award, they must have conferred on him authority to do so. Again, once the compromise award is made, the arbitrator becomes *functus officio*.

DELAYS AND DEFAULT

One of the advantages that arbitration often has over litigation is speed. One individual or group of arbitrators will have exclusive seisin of the dispute from the very beginning and may be available at short notice to dispose of all interlocutory applications and be expert in the subject matter of the dispute.

Respondent's delays Where the delay is on the respondent's part, the tribunal can take appropriate steps to speed matters up, if requested to do so. Arbitrators do not have inherent authority to make a default award, that is, find in the claimant's favour because the respondent has not defended the claim or has disregarded interlocutory orders made against him. But where such directions have not been complied with, an arbitrator can simply fix a date for the hearing, notify the respondent and hear the matter on the appointed date. A respondent may then come in and seek an adjournment, which the arbitrator may grant on strict terms.[29]

---

28   See post pp. 99-100.
29   Cf. *Grangeford Securities Ltd v. S.H. Ltd* [1990] ILRM 277.

Claimant's delays   It is less common for delays being caused by claimants, who ordinarily will be anxious to secure their redress at the earliest possible date. Where the claimant does delay unduly, the tribunal would be favourably disposed to an application to have the reference speeded up, by fixing a time within which directions must be complied with and setting a date for the hearing.

PRE-HEARING REVIEW

Where the reference is a somewhat complex affair, a pre-hearing review may be advisable in order to ensure that the actual hearing is conducted expeditiously and effectively. By this stage, discovery should have been completed and all witness statements and expert's reports should have been exchanged. The following matters should be addressed at this review:

i. Whether all previous directions have been complied with.

ii. Whether any further directions are needed, e.g. additional discovery, a meeting of the expert witnesses.

iii. Confirm what are the issues between the party and seek agreement on the order in which they should be dealt.

iv. Consider what issues should be addressed initially and be the subject of an interim award.

v. Set out a programme for the hearing, to reduce as much as possible inconvenience for the various witnesses, who may be travelling a considerable distance to the tribunal.

vi. Arrange that a list of the issues and the necessary bundles of documents are given to the arbitrator in sufficient time to read them before the hearing commences.

7

THE HEARING

The arbitrator will have notified the parties of the time and place of the hearing and will have endeavoured to find a location and timing which is as convenient as reasonably possible for all the parties. Careful consideration should be given to any proposal that all or part of the reference should be heard abroad because to do so might affect the law governing the conduct of the reference and give foreign courts some supervisory jurisdiction. It is advisable to have the consent of the parties to going abroad and their agreement about the governing law.

A significant number of arbitrations are conducted without any adversary-type hearing taking place. For instance, the arbitrator may just go and inspect the goods in a quality dispute. It may be a 'documents-only' arbitration; the reference may be conducted by the evidence and argument being submitted entirely by correspondence. Where there are two arbitrators, they may simply discuss the matter hoping to reach agreement. At law, however, it is required that a hearing takes place unless the parties agreed otherwise, expressly or by implication. Where a party has agreed to waive a hearing, it is an open question whether he can then change his mind and insist on a hearing taking place.

MINIMUM REQUIREMENTS

Although there are certain minimum standards that arbitration hearings are expected to comply with, these can be waived by agreement of the parties. Frequently the parties will opt for a far more informal way of conducting the reference or for an inquisitorial rather than an adversarial approach. With regard to implied waiver of certain procedural matters that are commonly treated as fundamental, the courts will insist on the clearest of implications. A court may reject some procedural devices as objectionable on the grounds of public policy. As has already been stated, the parties to the dispute must be given a 'fair trial' and the principles summed up in the maxims *audi alteram partem* and *nemo iudex in sua causa* must be observed, unless the parties clearly agreed otherwise, subject to public policy.

According to Mustill & Boyd,[1] the following are the minimum requirements of a hearing

1. Notice of hearing—each party must have notice that the hearing is to take place. It is the arbitrator's responsibility to ensure that the parties are properly notified, to avoid any misunderstandings.

2. Opportunity to attend—each party must have reasonable opportunity to be present at the hearing, together with his advisers and witnesses. While arbitrators will seek to convenience the parties, there are limits to their convenience; the arbitrator's obligation is to balance the legitimate interests of each party against the general purposes of arbitration, which is to provide a speedy method of resolving disputes.

3. Present throughout the hearing—each party must have the opportunity to be present throughout the entire hearing.

4. Present evidence and argument—each party must have a reasonable opportunity to present evidence and argument in support of his own case.

5. Controvert opponent's case—each party must have a reasonable opportunity to test his opponent's case by cross-examining witnesses, presenting rebutting evidence and addressing oral argument. In particular, unless there is agreement to the contrary, the arbitrator should not hear evidence or argument in the absence of one party and, generally, should not take the evidence himself in the absence of the two parties. The type of arbitration in question and the general understanding of how formal or otherwise it is supposed to be will indicate the parameters of this right to contradict the other party's case.

6. Oral hearing exhaustive—unless it is otherwise expressly agreed, the parties must present the whole of their evidence and their entire argument at the hearing.

Additionally, the entire matter must be dealt with in private; one of the main attractions of arbitration is that the press and members of the general public have no right to attend the hearing or to know the contents of the ultimate award.

---

1   *Commercial Arbitration* at pp. 302 et seq.

SPLITTING THE ISSUES

Usually, there will be two main issues, of liability and, if a party is found liable, the amount of compensation to be paid. At times there may be additional major issues. Often in such cases, it is more economical and convenient to split some of the issues and deal with one or more first, and then make an interim award. For example, if liability is rejected then the question of quantum cannot arise.

EX PARTE PROCEEDINGS

As has been observed, where a party has not entered a defence or has been in default of an interlocutory order, that does not entitle an arbitrator to find in favour of the other party—unless, of course, their agreement provides otherwise. Nor should an arbitrator proceed directly to his award when the respondent or his representative does not attend the hearing. Instead, from the material before him he must be satisfied that the claimant has made out a prima facie case; usually this will require hearing the claimant's evidence and arguments, and account must be taken of any matters put by the respondent on previous occasions.

For instance, in *Grangeford Securities Ltd v. S.H. Ltd*,[2] an arbitrator was appointed to decide a building dispute and he gave various directions. Those were not carried out by the respondent and there were many delays on his part. About a year following the appointment, the arbitrator fixed a day for the hearing. On that date the respondent sought an adjournment and the matter was peremptorily adjourned until that afternoon. When the tribunal then insisted on going ahead with the reference and would not adjourn it any longer, the respondent protested and left. But the tribunal then heard the evidence *ex parte* and made its award in favour of the claimant. It was held that the arbitrator had not acted improperly in the circumstances. McCarthy J summed up the principle as follows

> an arbitrator has an inherent power to issue directions requiring the parties to submit details of their claim or claims, to fix a date or dates for the hearing of the reference and, in a proper case, to proceed on such date or dates despite the absence of one or other party, where such party has been refused any further adjournment. There is no sanction that the arbitrator can properly impose upon a party to a reference where he has failed to present his claim in a formal fashion or refuses

2   [1990] ILRM 277.

to participate in the hearing. To proceed in his absence is not a punishment no more than it is such to make an award in such circumstances.[3]

ORDER OF EVENTS

As has been observed, the conduct of the hearing can vary from extreme informality to court-style procedures, depending on the nature of the dispute and the type of arbitration involved. For instance, if it is a documents-only reference, all that is needed is for the parties to give the arbitrator all of the requisite documents and he then will consider them and give his verdict in due course.

In the more formal kind of arbitration, especially where lawyers are involved, the hearing will commence with the claimant's representative outlining his case to the tribunal. How comprehensive that opening speech should be depends on how much the tribunal already knows about the dispute. For instance if the tribunal has seen a detailed statement of case and also written statements and copies of the principal relevant documents, the speech can be relatively brief and to the point—unless, of course, the tribunal has not had time to consider these documents.

The claimant's witnesses will then give their evidence. Normally, this will be given in answer to questions from the claimant's lawyer, who may not ask 'leading questions'. These are questions expressed in such a way as suggest what the answer should be. At times this evidence may be given in the form of written proofs rather than orally.

That witness may then be cross-examined by the opponent's representative. The main purpose of cross-examination is to test the accuracy of the evidence already given and, at times, to cast doubts on the very credibility of that witness. Even though in his evidence in chief a witness may have given a very convincing account of the relevant facts, after a skilful cross-examination his entire story may have lost most of its conviction. Contradictions between his evidence and what other witnesses say may defy explanation and the witness's powers of observation and of recall may be placed in doubt. On the other hand, if a witness stands up to a thorough cross-examination, his evidence will carry considerable weight.

Often that witness will be re-examined by his own party's representative. The purpose of re-examination is to rectify apparent damage to the case done during the course of cross-examination. Questions in re-ex-

---

3   Id. at p. 285.

amination are confined to matters which arose during the cross-examination.

A general point can be made about arbitrators interrupting the questioning of witnesses. They are exhorted not to intervene, especially during a cross-examination being conducted by a competent counsel. If matters require clarification, it may be best to leave them until the re-examination has ended and to then put the matter to the witness or the legal representative. Since the procedure is adversarial and not inquisitorial, the arbitrator should refrain from himself pursuing a lengthy line of enquiry. If a cross-examination becomes unduly aggressive, the arbitrator should intervene to protect the witness from being bullied.

The respondent's representative will then put his case in the same way—a brief opening statement followed by an examination in chief and re-examining any of his witness who were cross- examined.

Final submissions will then be made, first on behalf of the respondent and then for the claimant. During the course of these the arbitrator may seek clarification of various points, regarding either the evidence or legal issues.

At times fresh evidence may come to light after the hearing has concluded. In that event, a party may apply to the tribunal to re-open the hearing and the tribunal has a discretion to hear and admit the new evidence. An unfair refusal to hear that evidence may be misconduct on the part of the arbitrator. If the arbitrator had not unequivocally indicated that the hearing of the reference has concluded, that discretion should ordinarily be exercised in favour of the applicant.[4]

Where issues of law arise but the arbitrator does not have legal experience, he may decide to state a case to the High Court.[5] Alternatively, with the parties' consent, he may appoint a legal assessor to advise him on the points in issue. The parties should have a say in the choice of that assessor and have an opportunity to make submissions directly to him. However, his task is at most to advise; ultimately it is for the arbitrator to make the decision, taking due account of all advice received from the assessor.

RULES OF EVIDENCE

Unless the parties otherwise agree, arbitrators can only decide issues on the basis of evidence which would be admissible in a court of law. As was once remarked, 'the courts do allow considerable latitude, in practice at any rate,

4   *O'Sullivan v. J. Woodword & Sons Ltd* [1987] IR 255.
5   See post p. 112.

to the reception of evidence by [arbitrators], but to say as a general proposition that they are not bound by the rules of evidence [is] entirely misleading and likely to produce very great injustice.'[6] If an arbitrator deliberately admits inadmissible evidence on an important matter, he commits misconduct and his award will be set aside or remitted.[7] To admit evidence which is inadmissible is an error of law, which can be appealed. Unless, however, that evidence would have had a significant effect on the case, the court is unlikely to remit the award.

The parties' agreement that the ordinary rules of evidence shall not apply may be an express term of the arbitration agreement or be otherwise agreed in advance of the hearing; also, during the hearing, they may waive application of those rules. The type of arbitration being conducted may amount to an implied agreement to exclude those rules; the less formal the procedure to be followed, the more likely an implication to by-pass the law of evidence.

One of the main evidentiary issues in arbitrations is the application of the hearsay rule to documents and proving their origin and contents.[8]

WITNESSES

Subpoena   Where a witness refuses to attend and give evidence at the hearing, s. 20 of the 1954 Act authorises the party to the arbitration to obtain a subpoena from the High Court, be it *ad testificandum* or *duces tecum*. Unless that witness then attends the hearing or brings with him the documentation requested, as the case may be, he can be punished for contempt of court. It would seem that subpoenas are rarely used in arbitrations. Under s. 21 of the 1954 Act, the court may order a writ of *habeas corpus ad testificandum*, to ensure that an essential witness who is presently being held in prison will attend to give evidence.

Evidence on oath or affirmation   Unless the arbitration agreement provides otherwise, s. 19(2) of the 1954 Act gives the arbitrator a discretion to take the evidence on oath or on affirmation. Taking evidence on oath is not common in arbitrations but, if a party wants some witness to be so examined, ordinarily the arbitrator ought to accede to his request. There are various commonly used forms of oath and affirmation.

6   *Re Enoch & Zaretzky, Bock & Co.* [1910] 3 KB 327, at p. 336.
7   See post p. 119.
8   See generally, C. Fennell, *The Law of Evidence in Ireland* (1992) ch. 9.

Section 22(1)(d) of the 1954 Act authorises the court to order that a witness in an arbitration shall be examined on oath before an officer of the court, for instance the Master of the High Court. That subsection also authorises the court to issue a commission of request so that a witness who is outside the jurisdiction can be examined.

Silence Presumably the common law privilege against self-incrimination and the right not to disclose certain other privileged matters[9] applies in arbitrations as in litigation. Apart from these matters, an arbitrator cannot compel a witness to answer a question, although he would be justified in taking account of the witness' silence when reaching his conclusions on the issues. The extent to which the High Court will assist a party in coercing answers from a reluctant witness remains to be resolved.

Expert witnesses In many arbitrations, the principal witnesses are experts in particular fields of technical activity, for example, engineers, surveyors, valuers etc. Often these witnesses will have given evidence in previous arbitrations and some of them may have even acted as arbitrators in the past. As has been observed, frequently statements or abstracts of the various experts' evidence will have been exchanged before the hearing, so that each party has a complete picture of the other sides' evidence. The arbitrator may even request the parties, through their experts, to draw up a schedule of the points on which they disagree and perhaps clarify the reasons for and the extent of such disagreement.

In civil law countries, the tradition in litigation is for the court to appoint its own independent expert, rather than having perhaps to choose between two rival experts giving conflicting evidence. If the parties to an arbitration agree, they may select a common expert or even authorise the tribunal to select an appropriate expert.

At times the arbitrator will have considerable knowledge of the area of expertise of particular witnesses. In that event, he has a delicate task in not in effect becoming a witness himself. If he is minded to take account of certain information he possesses, he ought to put these facts to the witness and invite comments on them.

---

9   See generally, id. ch. 7.

8

THE AWARD

The decision of the tribunal is called an award, which resembles the orders made by a court when it desides a case. Additionally, the tribunal may give the reasons for the decision which it has reached, which resembles the reasoned judgment given by courts. There is no set format for making awards but, unless they are interim rulings, they should deal with all the issues in dispute with finality. The reliefs which an arbitral tribunal may order are almost as extensive as those which can be ordered by a court and usually the tribunal can make an order regarding the costs of the reference as well.

INTERIM AWARD

At times the tribunal may rule on certain aspects of the case, in the form of an interim award, before addressing the remaining issues. Especially if the issues are clearly separable and a finding on one or some of them would render it unnecessary to deal with the others, or those others may have to be dealt with in a radically different manner, it may be in the interests of the parties for some of the issues to be first adjudicated on. In the light of that interim ruling, the parties can then consider how the remainder of the reference is to be conducted. Where the outcome of the dispute would turn on what view the tribunal took of a point of law, there is much to be said for an interim award on the legal issue alone. Where a *Calderbank* offer has been made the arbitrator will usually be asked to make his award on liability and quantum on an interim basis and leave over the question of costs for a final award.

Arbitrators, however, are constantly cautioned against too readily making interim awards. Because it can happen that, on closer examination, the apparently simple interim solution does not satisfactory deal with the issues; what was hoped would save time and expense may turn out to be a more protracted and costly exercise than if all the issues had been dealt with together in a single final award.

Interim special case stated   One of the methods of in effect appealing an arbitrator's award in the courts is the special case stated procedure in s. 35(1)(b) of the 1954 Act. Under this, as is explained in Chapter 10,[1] the award will set out the findings of fact and will then pose certain questions of law arising from those conclusions, together with two or more findings in the alternative. This procedure can also be followed with interim awards; the arbitrator sets out his findings on some of the facts (which will bind the parties) and then poses related questions for the court to rule on, with alternative directions.

Consultative case stated   Instead of making an interim finding on a disputed issue of law, the tribunal may wish to have the High Court's guidance on the matter. In that event, s. 35(1)(a) of the 1954 Act provides for the consultative case stated, whereby the arbitrator can refer 'any question of law arising in the course of the reference' to the court. Here the tribunal will set out the relevant facts it has found and will then pose the question or questions of law at issue. But this statement of the facts is not an adjudication; it is not an interim award and accordingly the parties are not bound by the findings set out in the statement. Even if the tribunal choses not to state a consultative case under s. 35(1)(a), it may in an appropriate case be directed by the court to do so.

FORM AND CONTENTS OF AWARD

The 1954 Act does not indicate how the award should be drawn up or what it should contain. Since, however, arbitration awards are not self-enforcing, the tribunal's principal concern should be to produce an award which will be enforced by the courts, if the winning party has to resort to the courts to secure the reliefs he was awarded.

The following format may prove convenient—

1. Refer to the arbitration agreement: date and parties

2. State the date and method of appointment of the arbitrator(s)

3. Outline the procedure adopted (documents only; if hearing, give the dates)

4. Summarise what the issues are.

5. Set out what facts are agreed or are common ground.

---

1   Post pp. 122-125.

6. Summarise the evidence given.

7. First issue of fact: I find as fact that . . . [Sometimes reasons are given]

8. Second issue of fact (continue as first)

9. First issue of law:
   Argument for Claimant. . . .
   Argument for Respondent. . . .
   I prefer the case for the . . . and [Sometimes reasons are given]
   I therefore find for the . . . on this issue

10 Second Issue of law: (continue as first). . . .
   I therefore find for the . . . on this issue

11. The overall result of my determination of these issues is that. . . .

   I therefore determine and award ———— with interest at ———— per
   cent from ———— to [*the date of this award or as the case may be*]
   I further award and direct that . . . shall pay my fees of £ . . . and the
   costs shall be paid by . . .
   [or: this award is final as to all matters except costs]

   This award is final as to all matters except costs
   Date: Signature:
                           Witness:

Formalities   While arbitration awards can be oral, almost always they are
written and signed by the arbitrator. Where the tribunal consists of two
arbitrators and they cannot agree, then generally it is the umpire who makes
the award in lieu of them. Where the tribunal consists of three arbitrators
and it is provided that none of them shall be an umpire, then the decision of
any two of them is the binding award.[2] It is a common practice, although
not compulsory, for the signature[s] to be attested by a witness, who also
signs his name.

The parties to the reference should be named and not just described.
Usually, the award will be dated; the date is particularly relevant for the
calculation of any interest that may have been awarded. Often the award
will contain brief recitals, which set out how the arbitrator was appointed
and the general nature of the dispute.

An adjudication   It must be clear from the award that the tribunal adjudicated a dispute between the parties—as opposed, for example, to expressing

2   1954 Act s. 17(2).

an opinion on their differences. This is best done by directing that a specified sum of money shall be paid to a party, by ordering that certain other things should be done or not done. Parties' entitlements should be expressed in bold declaratory statements. In other words, the core of the award is modelled to an extent on the orders of a court drawn up by the registrar after the judge has given his reasoned judgment.

Complete   A final award should determine all of the issues that called for adjudication. Awards which decide only some of the issues in the dispute will not be maintained, nor will awards which are uncertain be enforced. Thus in *Kingston v. Layden*,[3] which concerned trespassing coal mine owners in Arigna, the arbitrator's conclusions were set out in detail and specified sums were directed to be paid by each party to the other, because both were found to have unlawfully entered on the other's property and taken coal from it. If the Statute of Limitations applied in the circumstances, each of these amounts would have been accordingly reduced. But the arbitrator did not rule on this matter; the award simply said that the question was 'subject to any decision of the court.' It was held that the award was not certain and could not be enforced. What the arbitrator should have done was to rule on the limitation point and, if wrong, his decision could have been corrected by the court. Alternatively, the question could have been put to the court in the form of a special case stated.

But is not essential that each and every issue in dispute is dealt with separately. Once it can be shown, from the award, that every issue was dealt with and was answered, that suffices. An arbitrator is permitted to make a single lump sum award in respect of a series of claims—unless, of course, he was appointed to decide them separately.

Where there are cross-claims, it generally is advisable to deal with each of them rather than simply awarding a balance of account. But the failure of the arbitrator to deal separately with a counterclaim and, instead, to award a single amount does not make his award bad. According to Hamilton J in *Stillorgan Orchard Ltd v. McLoughlin & Harvey Ltd*[4] an award will be sustained even though the arbitrator has 'omitted in his award to notice some claim put forward by a party if, according to the fair interpretation of the award, it is to be presumed that the arbitrator is taking the claim into his consideration in making his award.'[5] This is because 'the courts are always inclined to support the validity of an award and will make every reasonable

3   [1930] IR 265.
4   [1978] ILRM 128.
5   Id. at p.135.

presumption in favour of its being a final, certain and sufficient termination of the matters in dispute.'[6]

Final   The award should not leave any matter to be determined later by some third party, nor should the tribunal reserve any matter to be decided later by itself. Unless the intention is to make an interim award, the arbitrator must make a final adjudication of the issues presented to him. Nor should there be any uncertainty in the award; if it is unclear what precisely was decided, the award will not be enforced by the courts.

Reasons   Except where stipulated for, there is no obligation on the tribunal to state the reasons for its award, that is, the factual and legal considerations that prompted the decision. But giving reasons does not invalidate an award and, indeed, the courts in some countries will refuse to enforce awards which are not motivated. It is possible that furnishing reasons is required by the Constitution. What tribunals at times do is furnish a separate document, which is not strictly part of their award, setting out their reasoning. Even where they do not give their reasons, arbitrators are advised to set out for themselves their reasoning before making their decision; doing that, rather than relying on intuition, greatly assists them in coming to the correct conclusion.

In a recent instance,[7] it was held by Flood J that where an unreasoned award is challenged in the normal judicial review procedure, if from the evidence it is clear that the party's case was given practically no consideration, the arbitrator can be required to give reasons. This decision is under appeal. The authorities relied on for the above proposition were administrative law cases but the application of those authorities to consensual arbitration procedures is somewhat questionable. The arbitration procedure in that case was statutory, which may give rise to different considerations.[8]

Special case   The tribunal may give its award in the form of a 'special case' to be decided by the court. Such an award will contain a complete adjudication on the facts and a statement of the questions of law being asked. It generally contains two or more alternative awards, to cover the various possible answers which the court may give. However, where there are a considerable number of possible outcomes, depending on the answers, the tribunal may prefer to state a case by way of an interim award or may simply

6   Ibid. See too, *Childers Heights Housing Ltd v. Molderings Ltd* [1987] ILRM 47.
7   *Doyle v. Shakleton and Kildare C.C.* (unreported 20 January 1994); see post p...
8   Compare *Manning v. Shackleton and Cork C.C.* [1944] ILRM 346

state a consultative case, or indeed a 'mixed' final/interim case. An award in this 'mixed' form involves the tribunal deciding each of the questions of law in the manner it deems correct and making an award accordingly; but adds that if the court disagrees with the conclusions, the matter should be remitted to the tribunal, for it to decide in the light of the court's answers.

RELIEFS

Arbitral tribunals can give substantially the same reliefs and remedies as the courts, except of course an award cannot be the subject of immediate enforcement measures in the same way as a judgment of a court. But application may be made to the High Court under s. 41 of the 1954 Act to have the award rendered enforceable as if it were a judgment.

Damages The commonest type of award is for damages or compensation, of a stipulated amount, to be paid. The amount payable may be stated in a foreign currency.

Declaration The award may grant declaratory relief, that is, declare what the parties' rights are. A danger with this relief is making a declaration about moot points which are not immediately relevant to the dispute. A form of award that can be valuable is a declaration that one party shall indemnify another for expenditure to be incurred, up to a stated sum.

Equitable relief Relief of an equitable nature can also be given. Section 26 of the 1954 Act empowers arbitrators, in the absence of any contrary provision in the agreement, to direct specific performance of contracts other than those relating to land or to an interest in land.

Of course, the award does not have the immediate coercive effect of a specific performance order; for it to have such effect, an application must be made to the court under s. 41 of the 1954 Act.[9] The same applies to any injunction that the tribunal might award; until it is enforced under s. 41, a person who disobeys the injunction cannot be punished for contempt.

Interest Under s. 34 of the 1954 Act, unless the award states otherwise, it carries interest from the time it was given at the rate for judgment debts.[10] Whether interest can be awarded down to the date of the award is a more complex matter. The general principle regarding pre-judgment interest is

9   See ibid.
10   Presently 8 per cent: SI No. 12 of 1989.

that parties are not ordinarily entitled to be compensated for the late payment of money which is owing to them.[11] But there are extensive exceptions to the principle.

The arbitration agreement or the contract which a party is found to have contravened may have stipulated for the payment of pre-award interest at a certain rate.[12] Also, interest may constitute special damages, that is, the interest charges may have been a loss which, in the circumstances, the party in breach either knew or ought to have known would be incurred.[13] Under s. 53 of the Debtors (Ireland) Act, 1840,[14] the courts and, in England it has been held, arbitrators[15] may award interest where a demand for payment of the sum owing was made in writing and claimed interest from the date of the demand to the date of payment. Under s. 22 of the Courts Act, 1981, the courts are given a discretion to award interest, at the judgment debt rate, in an appropriate case and the question remains whether arbitrators have similar powers. These two discretionary powers to award interest apply only where an award of money is being made.

In *McStay v. Assicurazioni Generali Spa*[16] the Supreme Court declined to decide whether, generally, arbitrators can award interest for the period prior to the award. It was held that, since one of the issues submitted for determination by the arbitrator was whether he had jurisdiction to award such interest, his decision on the matter was final and could not be upset by the court—except, of course, where the issue was contained in a case stated to the court or there was an error of law on the record or misconduct. In this instance the arbitrator, an eminent Senior Counsel, found that he did not have authority to direct payment of pre-award interest. O'Flaherty J expressed the view that neither the common law generally nor s. 22 of the 1981 Act authorise arbitrators to award such interest, but found that the arbitration agreement there granted that power.

It has been held in Britain that, under a provision similar to s. 22 of the Courts Act, 1981, arbitrators now have the same powers as courts of record to award interest for the period prior to the award being made.[17] A similar approach was adopted in Australia.[18] But it was also held in Britain that if

11　*London Chatham & Dover Rly. Co. v. South Eastern Rly. Co.* [1983] AC 29.
12　Cf. Bills of Exchange Act, 1882, s. 57.
13　*Dods v. Coopers Creek Vineyards Ltd* [1987] 1 NZLR 530. Cf. *Hungerfords v. Walker*, 84 ALJLR 119 (1989).
14　3 & 4 Vic. c. 107.
15　*Chandris v. Isbrandtsen-Moller Co.* [1951] 1 KB 240 and *Food Corp. of India v. Marastro Co. Naviera SA* [1987] 1 WLR 134.
16　[1991] ILRM 237.
17　*President of India v. La Pintada Co. Navigacion S.A.* [1985] AC 104.
18　*Government Insurance Office v. Atkinson-Leighton*, 31 ALR 193 (1980).

the sum owing is paid late by the party in default then interest cannot be awarded under this power.[19]

COSTS

There are two kinds of costs in an arbitration. One is the costs of the award, that is, the tribunal's own remuneration and out of pocket expenses. As has been explained, each party to the reference is liable to pay these costs, although at times arbitrators may experience some difficulty in actually recovering the money. The other kind are the costs of the reference, that is, the expenses incurred by each party in preparing and presenting their case, for example, lawyers' fees, payments to witnesses etc.

Occasionally, the arbitration agreement will state how costs are to be dealt with. Even then, s. 30 of the 1954 Act declares void any stipulation that the parties shall bear their own costs, regardless of the outcome. But this prohibition does not apply to an *ad hoc* reference of a dispute which has already arisen. Sections 29-34 of the 1954 Act contain several provisions regarding costs and fees in arbitrations, which may be supplemented by whatever the parties agreed.

Arbitrator's discretion Normally arbitrators decide which party must pay the costs and the proportion to be so paid. But in an appropriate case, the award may contain no order regarding costs—other than for the arbitrator's own fees and disbursements, which then would be borne equally by the parties. Unless the parties agreed otherwise, s. 29(1) of the 1954 Act gives arbitrators a discretion over who shall bear the costs of the award and of the reference and the manner in which those costs or any part of them shall be paid. On several occasions it has been stressed that this discretion must be exercised judicially, meaning in this context that the arbitrator should normally follow the approach adopted in the High Court. And the court's general approach is that the 'costs follow the event', that is, whoever looses the reference should pay the costs incurred by the opposing party including the costs of the award.

In the *Everglade Maritime* case,[20] where the general approach to costs was extensively analysed, the court explained that, where parties opt for arbitration in England, that includes in accordance with the traditional

---

19 *La Pintada* case, supra n. 17.
20 *Everglades Maritime Inc. v. Schiffahrtsgellschaft Detleff von Appen mbH* [1993] QB 780.

English approach to costs. The principal features of that approach were summarised as follows:

> (1) The award of costs is in the discretion of arbitrators as it is of judges. (2) But in neither case is the discretion absolute or unfettered; it should be exercised judicially and according to settled principles. (3) The dominant principle is that, in the absence of circumstances justifying some other order, costs should follow the event so that the winner recovers his taxed or agreed costs and the loser pays them. (4) It is necessary to consider the outcome of the proceedings to decide what the event is which costs should follow. (5) In court proceedings the court will take account of a payment into court in exercising its discretion on costs: if a plaintiff does not recover more than was paid in he will ordinarily be ordered to pay the defendant's costs after the date of payment in. (6) A sealed offer is the arbitral equivalent of making a payment into court:[21]

Not following the 'event'   There are circumstances where a court or an arbitrator is justified in departing from the 'follow the event' principle. One is where the value of the claim is grossly exaggerated. But the fact that the claimant did not recover all that he sought is not ordinarily enough to justify such a departure. Another is where much time and attention were spent on certain issues, which the eventually successful party lost. Similarly, where a party was extravagant in the number of counsel or witnesses employed for the hearing. If a party has conducted himself in an unreasonable manner, which has unnecessarily prolonged the hearing or increased the other side's costs, he faces a costs penalty even though he 'won'.

Sealed offers   As in litigation, often a party will offer to settle the claim or counter-claim being brought against him. Usually those offers are made prior to the hearing commencing and normally are on a 'no prejudice' basis. Because there is no arbitration equivalent to lodging funds in court, offers may be made by giving the arbitral tribunal a sealed envelope containing the offer in question. Arbitrators must not look at 'without prejudice' offers until they have decided on the merits of the reference. If they knew what was offered, there is a distinct likelihood that the sum on offer might improperly influence their decision on the merits.

Where the sum offered in settlement exceeds the amount which the tribunal awards to the offeree, then generally the costs will be given in favour of the offeror. Those costs given are the costs incurred since the offer

---

21   Id. at p. 789.

was made. The rationale for this is that, 'in considering what is the relevant "event" in the period following the rejection of the offer, the claimant can be regarded as successful if he recovers a greater sum than the rejected offer and unsuccessful if he recovers a sum which is less than or is equal to the offer.'[22]

Calderbank offers   What is commonly referred to as a *Calderbank* offer is a sealed offer which is marked 'without prejudice save as to costs'. This kind of an offer can be opened by the arbitrator once he has made his award on the substantive issues in dispute. Accordingly, when these offers are made, the practice is to make an interim award on the merits of the case, leaving it to the parties for the time being to reach agreement on the costs, in the light of that award.[23] If they cannot agree, then the arbitrator decides on the costs, taking into account the contents of the *Calderbank* offer.

Offer including interest   Often interest on the amount claimed can constitute a very significant element of the claim. Settlement offers, therefore, may state a particular sum plus interest. In the *Transmountana Amadera* case,[24] the court set out how the interest element should be dealt with when calculating costs:

> The arbitrator knows what the claimant would have received if he had accepted the offer [which did not include interest]. The arbitrator knows what he has in fact awarded to the claimant both by way of principal and interest. In order that like should be compared with like, the interest element must be recalculated as if the award had been made on the same date as the offer. Alternatively, interest for the period between the offer and the award must notionally be added to the amount of the sealed offer. But subject to that the question [of whether the offer exceeded the award] is easily answered.[25]

Offer including costs   Exceptionally, an offer of settlement may include all or part of the opponent's costs incurred in the arbitration. The issue in the *Everglade Maritime* case[26] was whether the tribunal, in calculating whether the offer exceeded the sum awarded, should take account of the costs part of the offer in much the same way as interest is considered. In that

22   Id. [1992] 3 All ER 851, at p. 858.
23   Cf. *King v. Thomas McKenna Ltd* [1991] 2 QB 480.
24   *Transmontania Armadora S.A. v. Atlantic Shipping Co.* [1978] 2 All ER 870.
25   Id. at p. 877.
26   Supra n. 20.

case, if the costs element were so included, the respondents would have won the 'event'. For practical reasons and on principle, it was held that the costs element should be disregarded when making the calculation. If account were taken of costs, that would considerably complicate the matters parties must consider when deciding to settle, thereby rendering settlement generally more difficult. Also, while interest is part of a claimant's entitlement in the reference, there is no prior legal right to the ancillary claim for costs.

Quantum disputes   In disputes which are entirely about the actual amount of money which a party must pay, ordinarily there is no question of that party having broken a contract or committed a tort. For instance, the question may simply be how much additional rent should be paid or what value to put on shares. In such cases, the 'event' is very different from that in the usual kind of dispute; there is no clear 'winner' and 'looser'. Where an offer is made by the person who must make the payment, the only question is how near was the sum offered to that awarded by the tribunal. The tendency seems to be that where the offer comes close to the sum awarded, a fractional award of costs will be made to that party. Otherwise, no order for costs will be made—except in the most unusual case where the amount offered and the sum awarded are identical.

Judicial review of award on costs   Judicial review, generally, of arbitrators' awards is considered in Chapter 10 but it is appropriate to deal here with the question of review of arbitrators' discretion regarding costs. Because of legislative developments in Britain,[27] post 1979 decisions from there are not entirely reliable as precedents in this jurisdiction. Often the potential scope for any review will be extremely limited when the award does not give reasons. Where an award is made in the form of a case stated and the costs depart from the 'follow the event' principle, arbitrators are exhorted to state the reason for their decision on the costs; if no reasons are given, the award will be remitted by the court for them to be stated.

Misconduct   The scope for judicial review of a final award in this context was summarised by Diplock J as follows:

> Two things are clear. . . . First, that the court has jurisdiction where it appears on the material before it that an arbitrator has exercised his discretion in a non-judicial manner as to costs, to set aside his award so far as it relates to costs. The second . . . is that it matters not whether

27   Arbitration Act, 1979.

the material on which the court comes to the conclusion that there has been a non-judicial exercise of discretion appears on the face of the award . . . or appears by affidavit evidence which comes before the court.[28]

If, on the evidence before the court, the arbitrator acted in a non-judicial manner, that is technical misconduct and the award will be remitted to be amended in the light of the court's findings. On the other hand, the mere fact that the court would have made a different ruling regarding the costs is not enough to upset the arbitrator's decision. To be set aside, his decision must be one that a court could not reach, not one it would not reach if the entire matter were before the court. As Donaldson J put it,

> In reviewing an arbitrator's decision on costs, it is of the greatest importance to remember that the decision is within his discretion and not that of the courts. It is nothing to the point that [a judge] might have reached a different decision and that some other judge or arbitrator might have differed from both. I would . . . not be entitled to intervene unless . . . the arbitrator had misdirected himself.[29]

Where there is a clear departure from the usual 'follow the event' principle and no sufficient reason is given for doing so, that 'gives rise to a rebutable presumption that the arbitrator has erred in law or acted in an unjudicial manner to an extent justifying the intervention of the court.'[30] While the arbitrator cannot be required to give his reasons (except in a case stated), he as well as the parties are free to put matters on affidavit either to support or to contradict his award of costs. Indeed, at times it can be clear from a non-speaking award whether or not the arbitrator acted non-judicially, for instance, where the claim was for an excessive sum.

Remit   Where there has been some essentially procedural mishap or misunderstanding regarding costs, the court will exercise its broad discretion under s. 36 of the 1954 Act[31] to remit the matter to the arbitrator. For instance, in *King v. Thomas McKenna Ltd*,[32] where a sealed offer of settlement had been made, counsel for the offerer mistakenly omitted to indicate, to the arbitrator or to the other party, her wish for the question of costs to be left over until the issues of liability and of quantum had been

---

28   *Heaven & Hesterton Ltd v. Sven Widaeus A/B* [1958] 1 WLR 248, at p.252.
29   *Transmontania* case [1978] 2 All ER at p. 875.
30   Id. at p. 873.
31   See post p. 125-127.
32   [1991] 2 QB 480. See too *Harrision v. Thompson* [1987] 1 WLR 1235.

resolved. A final award was made against the offeror, including the costs of the reference. It was held that the court had jurisdiction under s. 36 to remit the matter so that the arbitrator could deal with the question of costs in the light of the offer.

Taxing costs   Where parties to litigation cannot agree on the quantum of costs awarded, the question is referred to a court officer, the Taxing Master, to decide the matter. Costs of a reference can also be taxed in this manner.[33] With the consent of the parties, however, s. 29(1) of the 1954 Act empowers the arbitrator to tax or settle the amount of costs to be paid. It often is preferable to leave the taxation to the arbitrator, because he would be entirely familiar with the great mass of documents prepared by the party and with the many other expensive inputs into the reference. Because he usually is an expert in the particular area of contention, he should be in an excellent position to judge what expense claims by the party are reasonable or are excessive. If taxation were left to the court, a taxing master might require considerable time to master the entire file before reaching conclusions.

Where the arbitrator is so empowered under s. 29(1) to conduct the taxation, he has a particularly delicate task when it comes to taxing the costs of the award, that is, his own fees and expenses. It has been said that he should fix his fees 'by reference to considerations which he can put forward and expect to justify as being reasonable',[34] for instance, the period of time he reasonably devoted to the work done and the scale of charges for the time he has completed.

Regardless of who conducts the taxation, ordinarily the costs are measured on a 'party and party' basis. This means that only expenses which were necessarily and properly incurred to advance a party's case will be allowed; in other words, the bare minimum to conduct the reference adequately. Very exceptionally the costs should be measures on a 'solicitor and client' basis, meaning the actual costs incurred, but not plainly unreasonable claims.

No costs order   Where the award contains no order directing the payment of costs of the reference, under s. 31 of the 1954 Act, any party may apply to the arbitrator to deal with the question. This application must be made within fourteen days of the award being published; thereafter, an application must be made to the court for an extension of the time to have the matter dealt with. The arbitrator must then hear any party who wishes to make

---

33   1954 Act s. 29(2).
34   *Government of Ceylon v. Chandris* [1963] 2 QB 327, at p.335.

representations on the issue of costs. He may then amend his award by adding directions regarding the payment of costs.

AMENDMENT

Where there is some minor error in a judgment or order of a court, it may be possible for the court to correct that error under what is known as the 'slip rule.' Under this, where a discrepancy is the result of some 'clerical mistake' or some 'accidental slip or omission', a party can apply to the court to make the necessary alteration. Section 28 of the 1954 Act provides a similar procedure for arbitrations. Unless the arbitration agreement provides otherwise, an arbitrator can amend his award in order to 'correct . . . any clerical mistake or error arising from any accidental slip or omission.' He cannot exercise this power of his own motion; one of the parties must apply to him and adequate notice must be given to the other party.

The slip rule does not allow an arbitrator to have second thoughts about any of the issues before him. Its purpose is to give true effect to his first thoughts and intentions, which were erroneously expressed in his award. If he assesses the evidence wrongly or if he has misconstrued or misappreciates the law, the matter cannot be corrected under this rule. There must have been some clerical mistake or the mistake was due to some accident. It has been held that s. 28 enables arbitrators to correct errors of accounting and arithmetic and even to award interest where the question of interest was inadvertently overlooked.[35] In *Mutual Shipping Corp. v. Bayshore Shipping Co.*,[36] when the arbitrator was taking notes of the evidence, he erroneously attributed the evidence of one party's witness to the other party. In consequence, he made his award in favour of the wrong party. It was held that even this error could be corrected under the 'slip rule'.

EFFECTS OF THE AWARD

Once a final award is made then, generally, the arbitrator becomes *functus officio* and no longer has any authority to deal with the matter. The exceptions to this principle are the s. 28 'slip rule', the s. 31 provision for where the award did not deal with costs and where, under s. 36, the court remits the award for re-consideration. Apart from these, s. 27 of the 1954 Act states that the award 'shall be final and binding on the parties and the

35   *Food Corp. of India v. Marastro Co. Naviera S.A.* [1987] 1 WLR 134.
36   [1985] 1 WLR 625.

persons claiming under them respectively.' In place of the successful claimant's claim under his contract, there is substituted an award which is enforceable in the courts, largely without reference to the underlying contract. Like judgments of courts of record, arbitration awards are *res judicata.*

Thus if a claimant subsequently discovers that the respondent's breach of contract or other wrong-doing caused far more loss than he had ever realised, he cannot make a fresh claim for the additional loss. Generally, all redress from a particular cause of action must be claimed for and dealt with in the one proceedings.[37] This principle can be waived by the parties, and the practices of a particular trade relating to this matter may constitute an implicit waiver. *Res judicata* applies to all matters decided by the award or necessarily involved in the decision.

Even if an issue between the parties does not meet this description, the courts have an inherent jurisdiction to prevent litigation or arbitration of an issue if it ought to have been raised previously in their case or their reference, as the case may be.[38] The basis for this jurisdiction is that it would be an abuse of the process of the court to litigate matters which really ought to have been dealt with in earlier proceedings between the same parties and related to the same subject matter. Parties should ensure that all possible aspects of their case are brought forward and should not be encouraged to hold certain parts back or to overlook some possible issues.

Nor, in any subsequent litigation or arbitration, can the parties dispute any issue on which they have failed in the award. Under the principle of estoppel, all issues of law or fact which were necessarily decided by the award cannot be reopened.[39]

Third parties to a reference cannot be affected by an award, unless they have agreed or assented to be so affected. However, s. 27 of the 1954 Act states that awards bind both the parties and all 'persons claiming under them. . . .'

ENFORCING THE AWARD

Once a person obtains a judgment of a court of record, he can take enforcement measures, for instance, registering a judgment mortgage, seizure by a sheriff under a *fi.fa.*, attachment of debts. An arbitration award is not directly enforceable in this manner. An award is indirectly enforceable,

37   *Fidelitas Shipping Co. v. V/O Exportchelb* [1966] 1 QB 630.
38   Ibid.
39   Ibid.

however, either by a party taking an action on the award or, under s. 41 of the 1954 Act, applying to the court to enforce the award as if it were a judgment. The enforcement of foreign arbitration awards is governed by Part V (ss. 54-59) of the 1954 Act and the Arbitration Act, 1980.[40] Arbitration is one of the matters not covered by the Brussels Convention on Jurisdiction and the Enforcement of Judgments, 1968, as amended.[41]

Seeking leave to enforce   Section 41 of the 1954 Act provides a speedy procedure for enforcing awards. A civil action in the High Court can be commenced by way of summary summons, grounded on an affidavit, seeking leave to enforce the award in the same manner as if it were a judgment and, where necessary, that judgment be entered against the other party in the terms of the award. Normally, it is not necessary to have a judgment in the terms but at times a judgment may be needed to enforce the award abroad.

The award must be in a form which is capable of being entered as a judgment. In order that an award fits this description, it may be possible, under s. 36 of the 1954 Act, to remit the award for re-consideration. Where the application for leave gives rise to conflicts of evidence on the affidavits, thus necessitating cross-examination and calling witnesses, and possibly discovery of documents and interrogatories, the application cannot then go ahead in the speedy procedure. Usually instead the court will order that the case shall proceed, as if it had been commenced by way of plenary summons, and will give directions regarding the further conduct of the case.

The grounds on which an award will be reviewed by the court are discussed in Chapter 10. In an action under s. 41 to enforce an award, it is not a defence to show that an application for judicial review would have succeeded, for instance because there is an error on the face of the award or some misconduct by the arbitrator. In such cases, the award is at most voidable but remains enforceable. But if it can be shown that the award is void, the loosing party has a good defence in an enforcement application. An award would be void where the arbitrator had no authority to make the award, for instance, his appointment had been validly revoked or he exceeded his jurisdiction. In *Grange Developments Ltd v. Dublin C.C.*,[42] Murphy J adopted the following statement of principle.

> Once an award has been made—and not challenged in the court—it should be entered as a judgment and given effect accordingly. It should

---

40 Cf. *Peter Cremer GmbH v. Co-Operative Molasses Traders Ltd* [1985] ILRM 564.
41 Cf. *Marc Rich & Co. v. Soc. Italiamo Impianti PA* (Case 190/89) [1991] ECR 3855.
42 Unreported, 14 March 1989.

not be held up because the loosing party says he wants to argue some point or other or says he wants to set up a counterclaim or anything of that sort. . . . [T]his summary method of enforcing awards . . . is to be used in nearly all cases. Leave should be given to enforce the award as a judgment unless there is real ground for doubting the validity of the award.[43]

If at the enforcement stage a party wants to raise a point which would be appropriate in proceedings to judicially review the award, he should seek to have the enforcement proceedings adjourned and apply to the court for leave to bring the review proceedings.[44] That may require an extension of time by the court to bring these proceedings.

Action on the award   Parties to an arbitration agreement impliedly undertake to perform any valid award that is made under that agreement. Where one party does not comply with the award, proceedings can be brought against him for breach of contract and to secure the redress given in the award. The plaintiff in such a case must plead and prove the arbitration agreement and the award, that the dispute was one within the terms of the arbitration agreement and that the arbitrator was duly appointed. There is a defence if the arbitrator's authority was revoked or if the award was void or exceeded the tribunal's jurisdiction. But it is no defence that the award is voidable and could be remitted or set aside.

---

43   *Middlemis & Gould v. Hartlepool Corp.* [1972] 1 WLR 1643, at p. 1646.
44   E.g. *L. Duggan & Sons Ltd v. Winkins* (Carroll J, 31 July 1987).

9

JUDICIAL CONTROL OF ARBITRATION: BEFORE THE AWARD

The whole purpose of arbitration is to have disputes resolved outside the ordinary court system. Yet arbitration is still very dependent on the courts, not only to enforce the ultimate award but also to intervene when something goes wrong in the course of a reference or to set aside or remit an award where it is demonstrably incorrect. It is necessary, therefore, to strike a proper balance between the autonomy of the arbitral tribunal and the supervisory powers of the courts. Too little judicial supervision renders arbitrators virtually a law unto themselves; too much judicial review frustrates the entire object of the process. It is convenient to deal first with controls exercisable before an award is made; those controls which can be exercised after the award are considered in the next following chapter.

In the leading modern authority on pre-award judicial control, the *Bremer Vulcan* case,[1] the general approach of the courts was explained as follows:

> The general supervisory jurisdiction of the High Court over the proceedings of inferior courts and tribunals extended only to bodies on whom Parliament has conferred statutory powers and duties which, when exercised, may lead to the detriment of subjects who may have to submit to their jurisdiction. These bodies would include arbitrators appointed to conduct a statutory arbitration ..., but they do not include arbitrators appointed pursuant to private arbitration agreement. In relation to private arbitrations, the jurisdiction of the High Court to supervise the conduct of the arbitration is confined to exercising the powers conferred upon it by the Arbitration Acts. ... The reason for this distinction is that the jurisdiction of an inferior court or statutory tribunal or arbitrator over the person who wishes to resist the claim is

---

1 *Bremer Vulkan Schiffbau und Maschienfabrik v. South India Shipping Corp.* [1982] AC 909.

compulsory whereas the jurisdiction of an arbitrator over both parties to a private arbitration agreement is consensual only.[2]

In very limited circumstances the courts will intervene, by way of injunction, to enforce or protect some legal or equitable right. Thus, conduct of the reference may be enjoined where the arbitration agreement was void or was voidable *ab initio*, or where the arbitrator otherwise has no jurisdiction to deal with the dispute, or where the agreement was terminated by repudiation or by being abandoned. Apart from these circumstances, a party aggrieved at the conduct or the outcome of a reference is confined to the judicial control methods provided for in the 1954 Act. But in the case of statutory arbitrations, where the tribunal is involved in the performance of some public function, it would seem that judicial review can also be obtained under R.S.C. Order 84.[3]

PARALLEL LEGAL PROCEEDINGS

As was explained in chapter 2, under s. 5 of the 1980 Act, where a dispute between parties is the subject of an arbitration clause in an agreement between them then any litigation arising in relation to that dispute will be stayed by the court, leaving it to the parties to arbitrate their differences. This stay is mandatory; the court has no discretion in the matter. Once however a party has delivered any pleading or taken 'any other steps' in the litigation, the proceedings will not then be stayed by the court.[4] In these circumstances, presumably the party who unsuccessfully sought the stay would be regarded as having waived his right to arbitration and the reference would not even be commenced. If he sought to commence the reference and appoint an arbitrator, presumably an injunction could be obtained restraining the conduct of a reference, pending the outcome of the litigation.

ARBITRATION AGREEMENT TERMINATED

If the arbitration agreement has been terminated then obviously neither party is obliged to participate in the reference. In such a case the court will make a declaration that the agreement has come to an end and, where necessary, may enjoin the purported conduct of the reference. While arbitration agreements have certain unique characteristics, their termination is governed by the general principles of the law of contract. According to the

---

2   Id. at p. 978.
3   See ante p. 15. Compare *R. v. Industrial Court, ex p. Asset* [1965] 1 QB 377.
4   E.g. *McCormac Products Ltd v. Monaghan Co-Op. Ltd* [1988] IR 304.

standard works of reference on contract law, contracts can be lawfully discharged principally by agreement or by frustration. While a contract can also be discharged by breach, the refusal of one party to honour his arbitration agreement no longer enables him to prevent the reference from being conducted.[5] A court will not direct specific performance of an agreement to arbitrate a dispute. Nor, it has been held, does the refusal by one party to perform all or part of the obligations he undertook in the arbitration agreement operate to bring that agreement to an end.[6] In particular, the prolonged failure by a claimant to prosecute his claim does not bring the agreement to an end.

Consensual termination As with all contracts, the parties can agree that an arbitration agreement shall come to an end prior to the time it originally was envisaged to run. No particular difficulties arise where that agreement is expressed. Parties also can impliedly agree to terminate their agreement, but their conduct must be such as unequivocally shows that intention, which was communicated to the other party and was accepted by him. Where a claimant in an arbitration has inordinately delayed, it is possible that in the circumstances the parties impliedly agreed to abandon the reference. The mere fact of delay, however, is equivocal, offering several possible explanations, and would not normally be treated as an agreement to terminate the obligation to go to arbitration.

In the leading modern case on implied termination of arbitration agreements, *Allied Marine Transport Ltd v. Vale do Rio*,[7] the test to be applied was held to be whether the party conducted himself so as to entitle the other to assume, and he did assume, that the contract was agreed to be abandoned *sub silentio*. In other words,

> if one party (O) so acts that his conduct, objectively considered, constitutes an offer, and the other party (A), believing that the conduct of O represents his actual intention, accepts O's offer, then a contract will come into existence and, on those facts, it will make no difference if O did not in fact intend to make the offer, or if he misunderstood A's acceptance, so that O's state of mind is, in such circumstances, irrelevant.[8]

But it was held that the failure to prosecute the claim in the circumstances there did not amount to a consensual abandonment of the arbitration because

5   1954 Act s. 9.
6   *Bremen Vulkan* case [1982] AC 909.
7   [1985] 1 WLR 925.
8   Id. at p. 936.

In the absence of special circumstances, silence and inaction by a party
to a reference are, objectively considered, just as consistent with his
having inadvertently forgotten about the matter; or with his simply
hoping the matter will die a natural death if he does not stir up the other
party; or with his office staff, or his agents, or his insurers or his
solicitors being appalling slow. . . . Exactly the same comment can be
made of the silence and inaction of the other party.[9]

It was also argued in that case that the circumstances estopped the
claimant from proceeding with the reference. Estoppel requires that a party
should have made an unequivocal representation that he does not intend to
enforce his strict legal rights against the other and detrimental reliance on
that representation. But mere delay does not meet these requirements. In
another case[10] an argument was made that there is an implied term in an
arbitration clause to the effect that the right to proceed with the reference
lapses after the expiry of a reasonable time during which the reference was
not proceeded with. But the court there expressed little enthusiasm for this
proposition.

Frustration   A contract comes to an end through frustration where there
has been so profound a change of circumstances from when it was entered
into that it has become physically or commercially impossible to perform
the contract, or performance would require something radically different
from what originally was envisaged. In the leading authority on frustration
in the present context, *Paal Wilson & Co. v. Partenreederi Hannah Blumen-
thal*,[11] it was accepted that a contract to refer a dispute to arbitration like,
any other contract, can be subject to the doctrine of frustration. For it to
operate, two requirements must exist:

The first . . . is that there must be some outside event or extraneous
change of situation, not foreseen or provided for by the parties at the
time of contracting, which either makes it impossible for the contract
to be performed at all, or at least renders its performance something
radically different from what the parties contemplated when they
entered into it. The second . . . is that the outside event or extraneous
change of situation concerned, and the consequences of either in
relation to the performance of the contract, must have occurred without either the fault or the default of either party to the contract.[12]

9   Id. at p. 937.
10 *Food Corp. of India v. Antclizo Shipping Corp.* [1988] 1 WLR 60.
11 [1983] AC 856.
12 Id. at p. 909.

It was held there that a protracted delay in prosecuting a claim did not amount to frustration because the delay was caused by the parties' default, not by the intervention of external causes.

Repudiation   A repudiation of a contract will only terminate it where the other party accepts the repudiation. Instead of acceptance, that innocent party can insist on the agreement being honoured, such as by prosecuting the reference in a arbitration.

LACK OF JURISDICTION

Where the tribunal does not have jurisdiction to deal with the dispute in question, a declaration to that effect can be obtained and also an injunction where appropriate. Of course the objecting party always has the option of waiting until attempts are made to enforce the ultimate award and then raise the jurisdiction point. However, it may be difficult to participate in the reference while having fundamental jurisdictional objections; also it can be most inconvenient to be deeply involved in the reference, especially when the court would seem to be in a position to stop it.

The granting of a declaration or an injunction is in the court's discretion; the mere fact that a party has a good objection to jurisdiction does not guarantee that the reference will be stopped. Among the matters which the court will take into account are the stage of the reference at which the objection was taken, how long the reference will be held up while the issue of jurisdiction is being resolved, how much of the matter in dispute is affected by the jurisdiction point if it is correct. It is unlikely that an injunction would be granted unless the jurisdictional point seems to be strong and parallel proceedings in the courts have been or are about to be commenced.

Another important consideration is whether the arbitrator is empowered to determine his own jurisdiction. If he has that power then once a question of jurisdiction is raised he may decide to refer the matter to the court, usually with the consent of the parties. If one party does not consent, the arbitrator may then leave it to the other party to commence proceedings. Even if the arbitrator is not so empowered, if the jurisdiction point would not substantially shorten the reference the court may suggest to the parties that they make an *ad hoc* submission to the arbitrator, empowering him to deal with the question of jurisdiction.

STALE ARBITRATIONS

A 'stale' arbitration means where a reference formally commenced but the claimant then does virtually nothing for some years. There are various reasons why claimants may choose to act in this manner, principally perhaps in order to ensure that any claim they may have is not shut out by limitation periods. The appropriate remedy for respondents in such references was the subject of very prominent and controversial litigation in England, where there was deep division among the judges on the matter and the solution adopted by a narrowly divided House of Lords was not universally welcomed in the arbitration community. It is pointless to speculate whether the Irish courts would follow the analysis of Lord Diplock in the *Bremer Vulkan* case[13] or would they follow the dissenting views of Lords Fraser and Scarman, which in the event were subsequently adopted by amending the legislation there.[14]

The case concerned a contract between an Indian ship-owner and a German shipyard to build five vessels. The contract was subject to German law but it provided for arbitration in London. In 1969 the ship-owner claimed damages in respect of several alleged defects. In 1972 an arbitrator was appointed and a statement of claim was delivered. Later, the parties agreed that some other alleged defects could be added to the points of claim. But nothing further was done about the arbitration; neither party ever applied to the arbitrator for directions. Then in 1977 the shipyard sought to put an end to the reference by commencing court proceedings seeking a declaration that the arbitrator had power to dismiss the claim for want of prosecution and also for an injunction restraining proceeding with the reference. Two issues, therefore, had to be determined; the powers of an arbitrator and the powers of the courts when confronted with stale arbitrations.

A court has an inherent jurisdiction to strike out actions for want of prosecution; this power 'is inherent in its constitutional function as a court of justice.'[15] Arbitrators, however, are not courts in that they are not subject to any constitutional obligation to administer justice and, unless they have contracted to do so, individuals cannot be coerced to submit to the jurisdiction of arbitrators. For this reason, it was held that arbitrators themselves do not possess any inherent authority to terminate a reference for want of prosecution by a party. For them to do so, they must be authorised by the

13   [1982] AC 909.
14   Arbitration Act, 1979, s. 5.
15   [1982] AC at p. 977.

terms of the contract or by statute, which was not the case there. In the absence of specific authority to do so, an arbitrator cannot even apply to the court to have the proceedings struck out.

There is an inherent jurisdiction in the courts to grant an injunction to protect a person's statutory, common law or contractual rights. However, there was no statutory or any common law obligation on claimants to proceed with reasonable diligence with the reference. The only possible legal source of such a duty could be the arbitration agreement. As regards delay in arbitration, there is an implied obligation on the parties to proceed with reasonable dispatch. But that obligation is mutual and goes no further than that the parties should co-operate in applying to the arbitrator for directions to unlock any impasse. As Lord Diplock put it,

> By appointing a sole arbitrator pursuant to a private arbitration agreement which does not specify expressly or by reference any particular procedural rules, the parties make the arbitrator the master of the procedure to be followed in the arbitration. . . . It is . . . a necessary implication from their having agreed that the arbitrator shall resolve their dispute, that both parties, respondent as well as claimant, are under a mutual obligation to one another to join in applying to the arbitrator for appropriate directions to put an end to the delay.[16]

The fact that the arbitrator cannot dismiss a claim for want of prosecution and that the court would not enjoin proceeding with a 'stale' arbitration does not mean that the respondent is helpless. The respondent can call on the claimant to join in applying to the arbitrator for directions. If the claimant did not co-operate in such application, the respondent could go ahead and so apply. The arbitrator would then give directions and if they were complied with, the reference would go ahead with the likelihood of the tribunal finding in favour of the respondent, who failed to appear at the time and place fixed. On account of the mutual obligation to co-operate in expediting the proceedings, undue delay could never amount to frustration of the contract, because frustration requires some supervening event and not the action or inaction of any of the parties. However, if in the circumstances it can be said that a party has abandoned the entire reference, there no longer is a contract and, accordingly, that party can be enjoined from insisting that the arbitration recommence. Similarly, a party who has repudiated the arbitration agreement cannot require the proceedings to continue.

16   Id. at pp. 985 and 986.

HOPELESS CLAIMS AND DEFENCES

There is scant judicial authority on the power of the court to intervene where the claimant's case is manifestly unstateable or where the respondent's defence is clearly hopeless. In ordinary litigation, the way of dealing with these situations is to apply to the court to strike out the plaintiff's case because it discloses no cause of action and, against defendants, to seek summary judgment on the grounds that there is no real defence.

Spurious claims   Theoretically, the award of costs to a respondent is his protection against being harassed by unstateable claims. However, costs, even assuming they can be recovered, never fully compensate a party for all the time and trouble involved in participating in a reference. It would seem however, in the light of *Bremer Vulcan*, that the court has no authority to intervene, either by stopping the reference going ahead or finding in favour of the respondent. His solution is to apply to the arbitrator to deal first with the net issue of law, viz. whether, on the facts alleged in the claim, there is a cause of action in law or even a *prima facie* case against the respondent. Where what is spurious is the facts being alleged by the claimant, there does not seem to be any especially speedy manner of bringing the matter to a head. A possibility might be to seek directions that the facts being alleged be set out in an affidavit.

Spurious defences   Usually the explanation for unstateable defences being put in is the respondent is seeking to delay as long as possible payment of the sum due, at times in the hope that the claimant would settle at a discount rather than undergo the bother of a reference. It would seem that the court has no power directly to assist the aggrieved claimant. One possibility might be to hold that there is no real dispute between the parties, thereby removing the stay under s. 5 of the 1980 Act. The arbitrator can always speed up conduct of the reference.

FRAUD AN ISSUE IN THE REFERENCE

If at any time during the course of the reference the question arises whether 'any party has been guilty of fraud', s. 39(2) of the 1954 Act authorises the court to either permit the arbitrator's authority to be revoked or to direct that the arbitration agreement itself shall cease to have effect. Because s. 39(2) applies only to agreements for the arbitration of future disputes, *ad hoc* submissions of an existing dispute involving accusations of fraud are not affected by the section.

What exactly fraud connotes in this context has not been definitely established. Its normal legal meaning is quite narrow, viz. deceit, that is, the knowing or reckless making of a false statement. The question is whether s. 39(2) applies to forms of dishonest conduct and sharp practices which do not meet the traditional definition of fraud.

The court's power to intervene in such instances is discretionary; in an appropriate case the court may leave the issue of fraud with the arbitrator.[17] It appears no longer essential to prove a *prima facie* case of fraud. Where the party being accused of fraud is seeking to have the matter litigated in public, the courts are very strongly disposed to either stop the arbitration or stay it.[18] Where the party accused of fraud still wants the charge dealt with in arbitration, the tendency is to leave the issue in the private tribunal.[19] But these principles are flexible and all depends on the circumstances of the case in question. For instance, who the arbitrator is and the nature of the fraud being alleged can be significant; some arbitrators are more competent to investigate frauds than others and some types of fraud are more closely connected with the underlying contract than are others. Also, there is a greater public interest in an open trial of certain allegations of fraud than in other types of dishonesty.

How this discretion should be exercised was considered in *Administratia Asigurarilor de Stat v. Insurance Corp. of Ireland*,[20] which concerned a dispute between an insurance company and its reinsurers, involving a large sum of money. The plaintiffs sought to repudiate their contracts and claimed that certain of the defendant's insurance arrangements had been of a fraudulent nature. It was the plaintiffs, alleging fraud, who sought to have the arbitration agreement set aside and they issued a summons and delivered a very lengthy draft statement of claim. The defendant then sought to stay those proceedings under s. 5 of the 1980 Act. O'Hanlon J stressed the width of the discretion the court has in applications brought under s. 39(2) of the 1954 Act; all the salient features of the case should be considered. The contention that a *prima facie* case of fraud must be established was rejected. Instead, it suffices if the allegations of fraud are 'made with perfect *bona fides* and with a deliberate intention of prosecuting them, and . . . there is no foundation for the contention that they are either sham or frivolous, or that they are put forward with the object of placing an obstacle in the way

17   *Administratia Asigurarilor de Stat v. Insurance Corp. of Ireland* [1990] ILRM 159.
18   *Russell v. Russell* (1880) 14 ChD 471.
19   Id. and *Cunningham-Reid v. Buchanan-Jardine* [1988] 1 WLR 678.
20   [1990] ILRM 159.

of a reference'.[21] The judge adverted to the established practice at the Bar, that Counsel will not sign pleadings which allege fraud unless satisfied that his client has substantial grounds for making that allegation. In any event, there was sufficient material before the court there on affidavit to make out a *prima facie* case of fraud.

Among the matters which leaned against continuation of the reference in this instance were the very magnitude and complexity of the claim; the difficult questions of law which were bound to arise; it was most unlikely that the parties ever contemplated claims of fraud being made under the arbitration clause; a hearing in the High Court, with an appeal to the Supreme Court, was preferable to a reference before two arbitrators from different jurisdictions, together with an as yet unnamed umpire, of unknown qualifications or abilities.

Under s. 39(2), where an issue in the dispute is whether any party has been guilty of fraud, the court may revoke the arbitrator's authority so far as may be necessary for the court to determine the matter.

STOPPING THE ARBITRATOR

There are several circumstances where the 1954 Act authorises the court to intervene in the reference by authorising or by ordering that the arbitrator shall no longer be involved in the matter. In such cases, the court may even go further and exercise its concurrent jurisdiction to put an end to the arbitration agreement itself.

Leave to revoke arbitrator's authority   Section 9 of the 1954 Act states that the appointment of an arbitrator is irrevocable; this prevents a party frustrating the conduct of a reference by purporting to withdraw the authority he had conferred on the arbitrator. However, s. 9 makes an exception and allows the court to permit a party to revoke his own arbitrator's authority. No indication is given in the section of when the court will allow a party to avail of this exception. As was observed in *City Centre Properties (ITC Pensions) Ltd v. Tersons*, this 'is a jurisdiction only to be used sparingly and in unusual cases'[22] because the party seeking to invoke s. 9 is in effect seeking to deprive the other party of his contractual rights, viz. to have his dispute resolved by way of arbitration. In an earlier instance, it was said that the court's power under s. 9 'ought to be exercised in the most sparing and cautious manner, lest an agreement to refer, from which all

21   Id. at p. 168, quoting from *Workman v. Belfast Harbour Cmrs.* [1899] IR 234, at p.244.
22   [1969] 1 WLR 772, at p. 778.

might hope for a speedy end of strife, should only open the flood gates for multiplied expenses and interminable delays.'[23] Leave under s. 9 might be given where the arbitrator has committed serious and irreparable misconduct, or is biased or very likely to be biased, or is otherwise unfit to carry out the reference.

Leave under s. 9 applies only to the arbitrator appointed by the applicant for that relief; it enables him to remove the arbitrator chosen by him. Section 9 does not authorise the removal of an arbitrator appointed by the other party. Where there is a sole arbitrator, appointed either by the parties themselves or some third party, it would seem that s. 9 applies.

Where leave is granted under s. 9, then the applicant can choose whether or not to exercise the power of revocation. A court order under s. 9 does not operate of itself to put an end to the arbitrator's authority.

Where the court gives a party leave to revoke an arbitrator's authority, on the application of any party to the agreement, it also may order that the arbitration agreement shall cease to have effect with respect to that particular dispute.[24]

Arbitrator's unreasonable delay   Section 24 of the 1954 Act authorises the court to remove an arbitrator who has 'fail[ed] to use all reasonable dispatch' in the conduct of the reference. What amounts to 'reasonable dispatch' for this purpose depends on the nature of the arbitration in question, the issues to be decided and all related matters. To warrant the arbitrator's removal, the delay must have been for some culpable reason on his part, because s. 24(2) provides that he is not entitled to receive any remuneration for his services.

Where an arbitrator is removed, s. 40(2) of the 1954 Act empowers the court to appoint a replacement; it also authorises the court instead to order that the arbitration agreement shall come to an end.

Arbitrator's misconduct   Section 37 of the 1954 Act authorises the court to remove an arbitrator who has 'misconducted himself or the proceedings'. Not all acts of what technically might amount to misconduct will warrant removal under this power.[25] The arbitrator must have said or done something which warrants one or both of the parties no longer having confidence in his being able to properly conduct the reference. For instance, in *Re Enoch Zaretsky Bock & Co.*,[26] the arbitrator insisted on being paid a substantial

---

23   *Den of Airlie S.S. Co. v. Mitsui & Co.* (1912) 106 LT 451, at p. 454.
24   1954 Act s. 40(2)(ii).
25   Cf. *K/S Norjari v. Hyundai Heavy Industries Co.* [1992] QB 863.
26   [1910] 1 KB 327.

sum of money before agreeing to state a special case to the court; ruled that a director of one of the companies involved should give evidence, even though he had no personal involvement in the issue in question; called a witness whom neither of the parties had called, who then produced as evidence copies of documents, which were inadmissible. The court there showed no hesitation in removing the arbitrator.

Where an arbitrator is removed from office, s. 40(2) of the 1954 Act empowers the court to appoint a replacement; instead, the court may direct that the arbitration agreement shall come to an end.

CONSULTATIVE CASE STATED

Section 35(1)(a) of the 1954 Act enables an arbitrator to state a consultative case on a question of law arising in the course of the reference. Especially where the question concerns a vital preliminary matter and resolution of it in one way would virtually put an end to the reference, the best course may be to state a case before making a final award.[27] Arbitrators have a discretion to state a consultative case and they can be directed to do so by the court. It would seem that the court will not readily compel an arbitrator to state a consultative case.[28]

---

27   E.g. *Hynes Ltd v. O'Malley Properties Ltd* [1989] ILRM 619.
28   E.g. *Dublin C.C. v. Healy & Shakleton*, Barrington J, 2 March 1984.

10

JUDICIAL CONTROL OF ARBITRATION: AFTER THE AWARD

An understanding of the present scheme for judicial control of arbitration awards requires consideration of how the system has developed over the years. Before the Arbitration Act, 1698, there was virtually no judicial control of arbitrators, which is not all that surprising when judicial control of administrative action as it is conceived today, that is, judicial review in administrative law, was very limited at that time. The prerogative writs of *certiorari*, prohibition, etc. existed and their function was to enable the courts to monitor the activities of subordinate courts, especially the magistracy. After 1698, when most arbitrations took place in the context of an agreement that the submission should be made a rule of court, the reference would then be sufficiently connected with the court for it to assert an inherent power to monitor its conduct and outcome. Furthermore, that Act commanded the court, where the submission was to be so ruled, to set aside and declare void any arbitration 'procured by corruption or undue means.' It must be most exceptional now for parties to agree that their submissions shall be made a rule of court but, where they do so, the court has inherent authority to review the award.

Two major innovations, the case stated procedure and the power to remit awards back to the tribunal, were adopted in the Common Law Procedure Amendment Act (Ireland), 1856,[1] and these still form a key part of the present scheme of judicial control. Unless the agreement provided otherwise, the arbitrator could make his findings of fact and then state a case to the court,[2] setting out questions of law to be resolved, together with alternative rulings depending on how those questions were answered. This ensured that the award would be consistent with the law. However, the arbitrator could not be compelled by one of the parties to state a case and the procedure did not apply to arbitrations which were not to be made a rule of court. The power to remit awards back to the arbitrator[3] was most

1   19 & 20 Vic. c. 102.
2   S. 8.   3 S. 11.

beneficial because it enabled errors to be corrected by the court. Without this power, the defective award would be bad and unenforceable and the parties might have to commence the reference all over again, at perhaps considerable expense and inconvenience. In 1889 legislation was passed[4] which greatly improved the machinery for judicial supervision in England but its provisions did not extend to Ireland.

Where the arbitration is part of a statutory process for resolving disputes, such as under the Acquisition of Land (Assessment of Compensation) Act, 1919, the proceedings are part of the public administrative law process and, apparently, can be the subject of judicial review under Order 84 of the Rules of the Superior Courts.[5] But in private arbitrations the courts do not possess equivalent supervisory authority, with the anomalous exception of granting *certiorari* to quash an error of law on the face of the award.

The legislators in several foreign jurisdictions have intervened to tip the balance very much in the direction of arbitral autonomy. For in England the Arbitration Act, 1979, both restricted further the scope of any judicial review and, in the case of certain international arbitration clauses, sanctioned the parties contracting out of practically all judicial review. There have been similar developments in Canada and Australia and in several European states. And in what perhaps is the most important international arbitration process, the International Chamber of Commerce's (ICC) Court of Arbitration, the parties to references under this procedure expressly 'waive their right to any form of appeal insofar as such waiver can be validly made.'[6]

Under the United Nations Commission on International Trade's (UNCI-TRAL) Model Law on International Arbitration, which is now adopted in many countries, the only grounds on which a court will review awards are stipulated as follows:

An arbitral award may be set aside . . . only if

(a) the party making the application furnishes proof that:

(i) a party to the arbitration agreement referred to in Article 7 was under some incapacity; or the said agreement is not valid under the law to which the parties have subjected it or, failing any indication thereon, under the law of this State; or
(ii) the party making the application was not given proper notice of

---

4   Arbitration Act, 1889.
5   E.g. *Manning v. Shackleton and Cork C.C.* [1994] ILRM 346. Compare *R. v. Industrial Court, ex p. ASSET* [1965] 1 QB 377.
6   Art. 24(2).

the appointment of an arbitrator or of the arbitral proceedings or was otherwise unable to present his case; or

(iii) the award deals with a dispute not contemplated by or not falling within the terms of the submission to arbitration, or contains decisions on matters beyond the scope of the submission to arbitration, provided that, if the decisions on matters submitted to arbitration can be separated from those not so submitted, only that part of the award which contains decisions on matters not submitted to arbitration may be set aside; or

(iv) the composition of the arbitral tribunal or the arbitral procedure was not in accordance with the agreement of the parties, unless such agreement was in conflict with a provision of this Law from which the parties cannot derogate, or failing such agreement, was not in accordance with this Law; or

(b) the court finds that:

(i) the subject-matter of the dispute is not capable of settlement by arbitration under the law of this State; or

(ii) the award is in conflict with the public policy of this State.[7]

Similar provisions have *not* been enacted in Ireland, except for the legislation which envisages disputes between friendly societies or industrial and provident societies and their members being determined by arbitration.[8] In the case of disputes decided under such arbitration arrangements, the award is made 'binding and conclusive on all parties, without appeal' and not 'removable into any court of law or restrainable by injunction'.[9] There have been no modern reported cases which deal with the scope of this 'ouster clause'.

THE PRESENT JUDICIAL CLIMATE

In the early part of this century, when courts were still somewhat suspicious of arbitration, they tended to scrutinise in some depth awards being challenged. Courts today are far less inclined to intervene and, on the question of judicial review of awards generally, it has been observed that 'great care has to be used in reading the decisions of a century or half a century ago' on these matters.

---

7   Art. 34(2).
8   See ante p. 15.
9   Friendly Societies Act, 1896, s. 68(1) and Industrial & Provident Societies Act, 1893, s. 49(1).

In recent years, the courts have demonstrated a marked reluctance to interfere with arbitration awards where it is alleged that the conclusions of fact or of law in them are wrong or are unsustainable. Some sixty years ago FitzGibbon J remarked that 'the trend of modern decisions has been in the direction of upholding, as far as may be reasonably possible, the awards of arbitrators and . . . a court should not be astute, as was the case a century ago, to set aside awards upon small and technical objections. . . .'[10]

Giving judgment in 1988 on behalf of the Supreme Court in *Keenan v. Shield Insurance Co.*,[11] McCarthy J observed that

> It ill becomes the courts to show any readiness to interfere in such a process; if policy considerations are appropriate, as I believe they are, . . . then every such consideration points to the desirability of making an arbitration award final in every sense of the term.[12]

In *Hogan v. St. Kevin's Co.*,[13] Murphy J expressed similar views, that

> Where parties refer disputes between them to the decision of an arbitrator chosen by them perhaps for his particular qualifications in comprehending technical issues involved in the dispute or perhaps for reasons relating to expedition, privacy or costs, it is obviously and manifestly their intention that the issue between them should be decided, and decided finally, by the person selected by them to adjudicate upon the matter. . . . The Court should be slow to usurp the functions of the chosen tribunal by intervening, whether by way of setting aside an award, remitting an award or directing a case to be stated.[14]

Grounds for intervention Bearing these considerations in mind, the main reasons for court intervention in private arbitration following publication of the award were summed up as follows:

> The courts will not interfere with the conduct of proceedings by the arbitrator except in circumstances which are now well defined. If the arbitrator is guilty of misconduct, his award may be set aside or remitted. If the award contains an error of law on its face, it may be sent back or remitted. If a special case is stated on a question of law, the court will determine that question of law within the framework of

10 *Kingston v. Layden* [1930] IR 265, at p. 289.
11 [1988] IR 89.
12 Id. at p. 96.
13 [986] IR 80.
14 Id. at p. 88.

the particular special case. But if there is no misconduct, if there is no error of law on the face of the award, or if no special case is stated, it is quite immaterial that the arbitrator may have erred in point of fact, or, indeed, in point of law. It is not misconduct to make a mistake of fact. It is not misconduct to go wrong in law so long as any mistake of law does not appear on the face of the award.[15]

Additionally, the court can remit an award where the arbitrator has committed some error in the discharge of his functions.

In the case of statutory arbitrations, where the tribunal is assisting the performance of some public function, it may be that the grounds of review are more extensive. Or in such cases, there may be some obligation on the tribunal to supply reasons when requested, even when the reference has come to any end.

Contracting out of judicial supervision Formerly the courts would disregard any agreement between the parties purporting to exclude or restrict the court's power of review under the Arbitration Acts. Such agreements, it was held, were contrary to public policy and accordingly were unenforceable.[16] It is debatable whether today the Irish courts would exercise their review powers in the face of such a stipulation, except perhaps where allegations of serious misconduct are being made against the arbitrator or the jurisdiction to remit is being invoked. Especially in international arbitration arrangements, contracts ousting the supervisory jurisdiction of the courts may no longer always offend against public policy.

So it was held in New Zealand in *CBI NZ Ltd v. Badger Chiyoda*,[17] which concerned the 'waiver' clause in the ICC's arbitration rules. It was held there that 'public policy . . . veers away from applying the *Czarnikow* approach to a commercial international arbitration where parties of equal bargaining strength have chosen to resolve their dispute under the rules of a respected international arbitration organisation with a retired High Court judge as arbitrator.'[18] Among the reasons given for reaching this conclusion were the growing dependence of New Zealand on international trade, the prominence of arbitration arrangements in international commercial agreements, especially ICC arbitration, accession to the New York Convention on the enforcement of foreign arbitration awards, the greater tolerance for

---

15   *Tersons Ltd v. Stevenage Development Corp.* [1965] 1 QB 37, at p. 51.
16   *Czarnikow v. Roth, Schmidt & Co.* [1922] 2 KB 478 and *Antrim Newtown Developments Ltd v. Department of Environment* [1989] NI 26.
17   [1989] 2 NZLR 669.
18   Id. at p. 694.

excluding review in foreign arbitration laws and the 'chauvinism implicit in the famous bon mot' of Scrutton LJ in the *Czarnikow* case.[19]

MISCONDUCT

The term misconduct in the present context is most inappropriate because of its connotation of wilful wrongdoing. Misconduct under s. 37 of the 1954 Act, which justifies the court removing the arbitrator,[20] may require a degree of personal impropriety. But s. 38 of the Act, which empowers the court to set aside the award for misconduct, includes 'misconducting the proceedings.' As well as serious breaches of the *nemo iudex in sua causa* and the *audi alteram partem* maxims, misconduct here includes acting without or outside jurisdiction—such as were there was no binding arbitration agreement, where the matters in dispute fell outside the agreement, where the relief granted lay outside the arbitrator's powers and where he was not validly appointed. Not following the general rules of evidence is misconduct, except where the parties excluded those rules.[21] It is misconduct not to hear relevant evidence[22] or not affording a party sufficient opportunity to make submissions on a material point.[23]

But making an error of fact or of law, or inconsistency of reasoning, do not fall under this heading.[24]

Nor, it has been held, is it misconduct for an arbitrator to refuse to state a case to the High Court under s. 35 of the 1954 Act. Because the power given by s. 35 to arbitrators is discretionary, it was held in *Stillorgan Orchard Ltd v. McLoughlin & Harvey*[25] that an arbitrator does not act improperly when he refuses an application by a party to state a case. But it would be misconduct for him to proceed to publish his award without affording that party the opportunity to apply to the court to order a case stated.[26]

Mustill & Boyd summarise what constitutes misconduct for these purposes as follows:

1. Failure to conduct the reference in the manner expressly or impliedly prescribed by the submission will (unless both parties consent) always

---

19   Quoted ante p. 9.
20   See ante pp. 51 and 53-54.
21   *Re Enoch Zaretsky, Bock & Co.* [1910] 3 K.B. 327.
22   *O'Sullivan v. Joseph Woodword & Co.* [1987] IR 255.
23   *Geraghty v. Rohan Industrial Estates Ltd* [1988] IR 419.
24   *Moran v. Lloyds* [1983] QB 542 and *Church & General Insurance Co. v. Connolly* (Costello J, 7 May 1981).
25   [1978] ILRM 128.

amount to misconduct, although not necessarily to misconduct which will lead the court to intervene.

2. Whatever the provisions of the submission, it is misconduct to behave in a way regarded by the courts as contrary to public policy.

3. Unless the submission expressly or impliedly permits, or unless the parties consent, it is misconduct to behave in a way which is, or gives the appearance of being, unfair.

4. For this purpose, fairness does not necessarily involve conducting the proceedings in the same way as an action in Court; regard must be had to the identity of the parties, and of the chosen arbitrator, and to the nature of the subject matter.

5. There are, however, certain minimum requirements—notably the hearing of both sides, and abstention from receiving evidence or argument in the absence of one party—which are regarded as essential to the fair conduct of the reference.[27]

Instead of setting aside the award on the grounds of misconduct, the court may remit it,[28] in which case a new award must be made within three months. Even though there was misconduct but the arbitrator could have come to no other conclusion on the central issues, the court may refuse to set aside or remit the award. Thus in *Geraghty v. Rohan Industrial Estates Ltd*,[29] the arbitrator indicated to the parties that he would split the issues and would first give an interim award on one of them. During the course of the hearing he decided not to follow this course but did not make it abundantly clear to the party's legal representatives that he had changed his mind on this matter. Although this constituted misconduct of the proceedings, the court refused to set aside or remit the award because, in the circumstances, the arbitrator's error made no difference. Similarly, where there was misconduct but the complaining party has taken the benefit of the award, the court may also refuse to set aside or remit the award.[30]

ERROR OF LAW ON FACE OF THE RECORD

For centuries the courts have had jurisdiction to quash determinations by public judicial tribunals were there was an error of law on the face of their

26 See post p. 122, n. 46.
27 *Commercial Arbitration* at p. 551.
28 1954 Act s. 36(2). E.g. *O'Sullivan v. Joseph Woodword & Co.* [1987] IR 255.
29 [1988] IR 419.
30 E.g. *European Grain & Shipping Ltd v. Johnston* [1983] 1 QB 520.

record. The courts also have had a jurisdiction to set aside the awards of private arbitrators on similar grounds.[31] In such cases, the court will 'look at the award itself to find whether it contains . . . some legal proposition which is the basis of the award and which you can then say is erroneous.'[32] Thus the fact that a transcript of the proceedings during the reference suggests that a mistake was made is not enough; the error must be in the very terms of the award or in documents incorporated in it.

In *Keenan v. Shield Insurance Co.*,[33] McCarthy J said that the test is one of 'obvious error'; whether there is an 'error of law so fundamental that the courts cannot stand aside and allow it to remain unchallenged.'[34] The extent to which a tribunal's lack of jurisdiction to entertain the reference, as contrasted with errors committed within the jurisdiction, constitutes error of law for this purpose has not been discussed by the courts. A decision by the arbitrator to exclude evidence is an error of law for these purposes.[35]

But where the error of law is with regard to a question expressly posed to the arbitrator and not merely arising incidentally, the court will not intervene. Thus in *McStay v. Assicurzioni Generali Spa*,[36] where the arbitration clause required inter alia a ruling on what interest if any was payable, the Supreme Court refused to review the award even if the ruling given was plainly wrong. The court distinguished between an 'error on the face' which arises 'where a general issue in dispute is submitted' for determination and an issue of law arises from a consideration of the issue and, on the other hand, 'where a precise question of law has been submitted.'[37] In the latter case, because the parties have chosen arbitration to resolve that very question, the decision will not be overturned by the court, no matter how erroneous it may be.[38]

Some interesting questions arise where an award is being contested because the underlying agreement between the parties was illegal. This point arose in *Church & General Insurance Co. v. Connolly*,[39] where it was contended that the insurance contract between the parties contravened regulations governing the insurance industry. The question of illegality had

31   *Kent v. Elstob* (1802) 3 East 18; described in the *Bremer Vulcan case* [1981] AC at p. 978 as a 'confessedly anomalous jurisdiction'.
32   *Honourable Irish Soc. v. Minister for Finance* [1958] NI 170, at p. 180.
33   [1988] IR 89.
34   Id. at p. 96. Cf. *O'Farrell v. Cochrane* [1991] 2 IR 513, where error was not established.
35   *Barnett Transport v. Davidson* [1991] 1 NZLR 121.
36   [1991] ILRM 237.
37   Id. at p. 243.
38   See too, *GUS Properties Ltd v. Tower Corp.* [1992] 2 NZLR 678 and *McMahon v. Heagney* (McWilliam J, 31 July 1991).
39   Costello J, 7 May 1981.

not been raised during the course of the reference but it was argued that to enforce an award based on an illegal contract would be contrary to public policy. Costello J's solution was to find that, if the illegality point had been raised at the hearing, the arbitrator would have had the jurisdiction to deal with it. If on the other hand the issue is first raised in a judicial review application, the court should canvass the question of illegality. If it then appeared that performance of the award would involve doing something unlawful, the question should be remitted to the arbitrator for his ruling. Presumably the court would set aside the award if the arbitrator had no jurisdiction to decide the illegality question. In any event, it is most unlikely that the court would ever order enforcement of an arbitration award requiring the performance of unlawful acts or payment of damages for not having acted unlawfully.

The court's jurisdiction to interfere on this ground has been described as both clumsy and capricious.[40] Once the award has been made the case stated procedure, described below, cannot be used to challenge conclusions of law; an aggrieved party's only redress then is this anomalous jurisdiction, unless of course the challenge goes deeper than simple error of law. Everything depends on how much detail is set out in the award itself or in documents incorporated in the award. The rules which determine whether any particular document is incorporated in the award can operate in a somewhat erratic way. Where, as often is the case in Ireland, the award does not give the tribunal's reasoning, it is only rarely that error of law will be disclosed.

In *Doyle v. Shackleton & Kildare C.C.*,[41] Flood J overcame some of these difficulties by holding that circumstances can exist where, after the entire arbitration has ended, the tribunal can be required to state its reasons for its award. The dispute concerned the value of land; according to the owner's witness it was valued around £1,377,000 but the purchaser's witnesses valued it at around £125,000. The amount awarded was £106,000. An application to set aside the award because it was so low to be perverse and irrational was rejected by the court; that the tribunal must have virtually disregarded the evidence tendered by the land-owner does not render the award perverse. However, as regards one aspect of the land, the value to be put on the residual surface of quarried-out land, Flood J held that there was '*prima facie* evidence of an inconsistent basis of calculation' of that land. Accordingly and because the arbitrator declined to give his reasons for his

---

40   *Mustill & Boyd* at p.585.
41   Unreported, 20 January 1994. Compare *Manning v. Shackleton & Cork C.C.* [1994] 1 ILRM 346

award, not even on affidavit to the court, it was held that the award should be set aside and a fresh appointment made. At the time of writing this case is under appeal.

In the past if the court found that the arbitrator had indeed erred, it had no choice but to set the award aside, so that the entire reference had to begin all over again. Now in an appropriate case the matter can be remitted to the arbitrator.

SPECIAL CASE

In 1856 the Legislature introduced a mechanism whereby the arbitrator's findings could be appealed to the courts on restricted grounds.[42] This is the 'case stated' or 'special case' procedure, now in s. 35(1)(b) of the 1954 Act, which permits an arbitrator to state his award in the form of a special case for consideration by the court.[43] An agreement between the parties to deprive an arbitrator of this option may no longer invariably be void as being contrary to public policy.[44] Section 35(1)(b) of the Act empowers the court to direct that an award shall be made in the form of a special case. Most court proceedings concerning the substance of awards take this form.

Once an award has been published, it is then too late to mount an appeal in this manner.[45] If, however, one party requests the arbitrator to state a case but he proceeds to hand down an award without affording that party adequate opportunity to apply to the court for directions, the arbitrator has misconducted the proceedings.[46] As a result, the award will be set aside unless the court considers that in any event there was no basis for a special case.

The party who is seeking to have a case stated is advised to make a formal application to the arbitrator. In *Stillorgan Orchard Ltd v. McLoughlin & Harvey Ltd*,[47] during his submissions to the arbitrator counsel for one of the parties referred to the possibility of stating a case on the correct interpretation of a clause in the contract. The arbitrator did not state a case. It was held that there was no misconduct by the arbitrator because he was never asked to state a case and, even if he were so asked, he had a discretion whether or not to accede to the application.

---

42   19 & 20 Vic. c. 102, s.8.
43   For a more detailed discussion, see the 1st edition of Mustill & Boyd, *Commercial Arbitration* (1982), Appendix 3.
44   *CBI NZ Ltd v. Badger Chiyoda* [1989] 2 NZLR 669; see ante p. 117.
45   *Hogan v. St. Kevin's Co.* [1986] IR 80. Cf. *McStay v. Assicurazioni Generali SPA* [1991] ILRM 237.
46   In the *Hogan* case [1986] IR 80 the plaintiffs got an interim injunction.
47   [1978] ILRM 128.

Often the parties will supply the arbitrator with lists of findings they believe should be included in his award. He then decides what findings to make, but should not add the evidence on which those are based. Invariably, there will be two or more alternative awards, to anticipate which view the court takes on the issue of law to be decided. Instead of the court setting aside the award and remitting it to the arbitrator to deal with the matter, giving awards in the alternative enables the court to straight away create an immediately enforceable obligation by adopting the alternative with which it agrees.

At the hearing, the court is confined to the facts as set out in the special case; extrinsic evidence will not be admitted to amplify or explain those facts.

Court directing special case The circumstances where the court will direct a special case, therefore, defines the extent to which the court will insist on scrutinising the merits of an arbitration. The court is not directly concerned with evidence and the conclusions derived from it; the parties selected a special private tribunal perhaps principally because of its deep knowledge of the context of the dispute. Special case is confined to questions of law, not of fact, although there is an uncertain border between where primarily factual matters become also issues of law.[48] In the *Lysland* case[49] the English Court of Appeal set out several considerations that should influence a court in deciding whether to direct an appeal in this form:

(a) the qualifications and experience, in so far as known to the court, of the arbitral tribunal, both in general and in relation to the particular dispute; (b) where the question is one of construction, whether the constriction involves consideration of any technical terms or against the background of any particular industry, trade or market of which the tribunal has some specialised knowledge; (c) in general, and also where the question of law is one of construction, whether the answer requires or would be assisted by recourse to statutes, decided cases or textbooks; (d) whether an authoritative answer to the question of law by the court is likely to be of assistance in resolving future disputes or in introducing a measure of uniformity; for instance the construction of provisions in standard forms of contracts or the decision of issues on which the court is informed that different arbitrators have taken different views; (e) the amount involved in the dispute or the importance of the decision to the parties for any other reason; (f) the

48 *Tersons Ltd v. Stevenage Development Corp.* [1965] 1 QB 37.
49 *Halfdan Grieg & Co. A/S v. Sterling Cable and Navigation Corp.* [1973] 1 QB 843.

consequences of the delay likely to result from the special case procedure with its possibilities of further appeals, together with the question whether there has already been undue delay, in particular by the party seeking the statement of a special case; (g) whether the court forms the impression on any material before it that the arbitration tribunal is likely to reach a conclusion which is wrong in law or that it has shown any tendency in some way to behave unjudically. This could arise in a variety of ways. There might, for instance, be material indicating that the tribunal did not appreciate that any question of law was involved, or that it had refused a request for a special case out of hand without being willing to listen to the grounds on which it was requested; similarly, if the tribunal had in some way indicated that it was accepting a submission or proceeding on a basis which the court could see was likely to be erroneous in law.[50]

There Kerr J was of the view that borderline cases should be decided against stating a case, whereas the Court of Appeal took a more interventionist stance.

Conclusions of law   Courts might be expected to show less reluctance to interfere with the arbitrator's finding on a point of law. Yet the Irish courts take a markedly anti-interventionist stance even on such questions. For instance, in *Hogan v. St Kevin's Co.*[51] the parties to a commercial lease in a shopping centre agreed that the amount of service charges payable by the tenant should be decided by arbitration and they appointed an accountant to act as arbitrator. It was a term of the lease that a certificate of the landlord's expenses, signed by its auditors or accountants, shall be 'final and binding' in respect of the matters so certified. The question then arose of the significance of this clause to the issues in the reference. To that end, the parties agreed to appoint an independent lawyer to advise the arbitrator on all points of law arising out of the reference and both parties were represented by senior counsel at the hearing. One of the conclusions in the award was that the landlord's auditor's certificate of expenses could be impugned to a very limited extent, and it was this question that the tenant sought to have resolved by way of a special case. An application for a direction to state a case was refused because, in Murphy J's words, 'at the end of the day, both parties were content to have the important point of law determined not by the courts but by an arbitrator and that notwithstanding the fact that he himself possessed no legal qualifications. Having adopted that course, it

50   Id. at pp. 851-852.
51   [186] IR 80.

seems that it would be unfair and unjust to permit the unsuccessful party to assert a right to have a decision of the High Court substituted for that of the arbitrator.'[52]

Findings of fact On account of the principle that is a question of law whether, on the evidence before the tribunal, the arbitrator could have come to certain conclusions of fact, to some extent issues of fact can be the subject of a special case. Where such an issue is the subject of the case, the court will not approach the matter in the same way as it would when considering whether a jury verdict was against the entire weight of the evidence.[53] As a rule, the arbitrator must not simply provide the court with a record of the evidence heard, together with one or more questions and alternative directions, depending on the answers. The arbitrator should summarise the evidence on which he based his conclusions and the court may accept extracts from the evidence given or a short transcript dealing with the particular point in issue. Because of the way in which arbitrators can deal with the evidence in setting out the special case, especially when the courts will defer to them on issues of fact, rarely will a directed special case succeed on the basis of insufficient evidence. Of course, if the evidence is not fairly summarised, the arbitrator commits misconduct.

REMIT THE AWARD

The other major procedural innovation in 1856 was the power given to the court to remit the award to an arbitrator.[54] Instead of setting the entire award aside or upholding an award possessing some unsatisfactory features, the court could send the award back to an arbitrator to make such changes as the court directs. That power, now under s. 36 of the 1954 Act, can be exercised where there was misconduct by the arbitrator[55] or an error on the face of the award,[56] and in the following cases.

Arbitrator's mistake The power to remit can also be exercised where an arbitrator has made some mistake in drawing up his award and he then wants to have the matter remitted. Today in cases of this nature, such mistakes can usually be rectified by the arbitrator under the 'slip rule' in s. 28 of the 1954

---

52 Id. at p. 89.
53 *Tersons* case supra n. 41.
54 19 & 20 Vic. c. 102, s. 11.
55 E.g. *O'Sullivan v. Joseph Woodword & Sons Ltd* [1987] IR 255.
56 Cf. *Barnett Transport Ltd v. Davidson* [1991] 1 NZLR 121, where in the circumstances remission was held not to be appropriate.

Act.[57] If however, the arbitrator is unsure whether the mistake is of a kind which warrants correction under the 'slip rule', an application can be made under s. 36 of the 1954 Act to have the award remitted so that the necessary change can be made. For instance, in *Mutual Shipping Corp. v. Bayshore Shipping Co.*,[58] the arbitrator had misattributed evidence by a witness for one party to the other party's witness; if that evidence had been correctly attributed, the award would have gone the other way. Because the arbitrator was not sure that the 'slip rule' applied in such a case, an application was made under s. 36 to remit the award. That application was granted. Where it appears that the arbitrator took an erroneous view of the law, that is not a mistake for these purposes.[59]

Fresh evidence   The power to remit can be exercised as well where additional evidence is discovered after the making of the award which might have affected the decision if that evidence had been adduced during the hearing. That evidence must be such that it probably would have a substantial effect on the outcome of the reference. But the matter will not be remitted where the party had the evidence in question but failed to use it, or he was aware of its existence but did not take realistic steps to obtain it or, through lack of reasonable foresight, he failed to realise the actual or potential existence of the evidence. Even where the evidence is entirely new and of significance, the court has a residual discretion not to remit the award.

Other grounds   Formerly it was believed that the jurisdiction under s. 36 of the 1954 Act to remit a case was confined to the four grounds—misconduct, error on the face, arbitrator's mistake and fresh evidence.[60] However, in *King v. Thomas McKenna Ltd*,[61] it was held that the expansive phraseology in s. 36 should be given its ordinary meaning and that there is a wider jurisdiction to remit. According to Lord Donaldson MR,

> the remission jurisdiction extends . . . to any cases where, notwith-standing that the arbitrators have acted with complete propriety, due to mishap or misunderstanding some aspect of the dispute which has been the subject of the reference has not been considered and adjudicated upon as fully as or in a manner which the parties were entitled to expect *and* it would be inequitable to allow any award to take effect without some further consideration by the arbitrator. [Section 36] is

57   See ante p. 97.
58   [1985] 1 WLR 625.
59   *Food Corp. of India v. Marastro Co. Naviera S.A.* [1987] 1 WLR 134.
60   E.g. in *Mennaghan v. Dublin C.C.* [1984] ILRM 616; accepted as the law by both parties' counsel.
61   [1991] 2 QB 480.

designed to remedy deviations from the route which the reference should have taken towards its destination (the award) and not to remedy a situation in which, despite having followed an unimpeachable route, the arbitrators have made errors of fact or law and as a result have reached a destination which was not that which the court would have reached. This essential qualification is usually underlined by saying that the jurisdiction to remit is to be invoked, if at all, in relation to procedural mishaps or misunderstandings. This, however, is too narrow a view since the traditional grounds do not necessarily involve procedural errors. The qualification is however of fundamental importance.[62]

In that case, a *Calderbank* offer had been made but the offeror's counsel inadvertently failed to indicate to the tribunal or the other party that the award on the main issues of liability and quantum should take an interim form.[63]

A case that is difficult to categorise is *Manning v. Shackleton & Cork C.C.*[64] where, on the main issue of the merits of the award, the court declined to intervene. On the question of costs, it seems that the arbitrator was not aware that, when making an offer, the respondent undertook to carry out certain works in addition to the sum tendered. Had he known about these undertakings, his decision on costs might have been different. Although the case did not fall within the 'arbitrator's mistake' or the 'fresh evidence' categories, Barron J ruled that the question of costs should be remitted so that the relevance of those undertakings could be decided.

Whether the grounds on which a court will remit a case are more extensive in Ireland is debatable. In *McStay v. Assicurazioni Generali Spa*,[65] where an arbitrator's decision regarding a claim for pre-award interest was challenged, Finlay CJ stated that where an arbitrator decides a question of law incorrectly, then 'the court may in its discretion and in particular cases where the decision so expressed is clearly wrong on its face, intervene by way of remitting the matter or otherwise in the interests of justice.'[66] However, the reference here may have been to the 'error on the face' principle and not the jurisdiction under s. 36 of the 1954 Act. None of the authorities on that section or its predecessors appear to have been cited by counsel and the authority cited in the next following paragraph referred to error on the face.

---

62 Id. at p. 491.
63 See too *Harrison v. Thompson* [1989] 1 WLR 1325.
64 [1994]1 ILRM 346, at pp. 353-354.
65 [1991] ILRM 237.
66 Id. at p. 243.

Arbitration Act, 1954

Number 26 *of* 1954

AN ACT TO MAKE FURTHER AND BETTER PROVISION IN RESPECT OF ARBITRATIONS. [*9th December*, 1954]

BE IT ENACTED BY THE OIREACHTAS AS FOLLOWS:—

PART I

PRELIMINARY AND GENERAL

1.—(1) This Act may be cited as the Arbitration Act, 1954.

(2) This Act (except subsection (2) of section 12 and Part V) shall come into operation on the 1st day of January, 1955

(3) Subsection (2) of section 12 and Part V of this Act shall come into operation on such day as may be fixed for that purpose by order of the Government.

Short title and commencement

2.—(1) In this Act—

"arbitration agreement" means a written agreement to refer present or future differences to arbitration, whether an arbitrator is named therein or not;

"the Convention of 1927" means the Convention on the Execution of Foreign Arbitral Awards done at Geneva on the 26th day of September, 1927, set out in the Second Schedule to this Act;

"the Court" means the High Court;

"the operative date" means the 1st day of January, 1955;

"the Protocol of 1923" means the Protocol on Arbitration Clauses opened at Geneva on the 24th day of September, 1923, set out in the First Schedule to this Act;

"State Authority" means any authority being—

(*a*) a Minister of State,

(*b*) the Commissioners of Public Works in Ireland,

(*c*) the Irish Land Commission, or

(*d*) the Revenue Commissioners;

"the statutes of limitation" includes any enactment limiting the time within which any particular proceedings may be commenced.

(2) References in this Act to an award include references to an interim award.

Interpretation generally

3.—(1) For the purposes of this Act and for the purpose of the statutes of limitation as applying to arbitrations and of section 496 of the Merchant

Commencement of arbitration

Shipping Act, 1894, as amended by section 46 of this Act, an arbitration shall be deemed to be commenced when one party to the arbitration agreement serves on the other party or parties a written notice requiring him or them to appoint or concur in appointing an arbitrator or, where the arbitration agreement provides that the reference shall be to a person named or designated in the agreement, requiring him or them to submit the dispute to the person so named or designated.

(2) (*a*) A notice under subsection (1) of this section may be served—

(i) by delivering it to the person to whom it is to be served,

(ii) by leaving it at the place in the State at which that person ordinarily resides or carries on business,

(iii) by sending it by registered post in an envelope addressed to that person at the place in the State at which he ordinarily resides or carries on business,

(iv) in any other manner provided in the arbitration agreement.

(*b*) For the purposes of this subsection, a company registered under the Companies Acts, 1908 to 1924, shall be deemed to carry on business at its registered office in the State and every other body corporate and every unincorporated body shall be deemed to carry on business at its principal office or place of business in the State.

State authorities to be bound

4.—This Part, Part II (except subsection (2) of section 12) and Part III of this Act shall apply to an arbitration under an arbitration agreement to which a State authority is a party.

Exclusion of certain arbitrations

5.—Notwithstanding anything contained in this Act, this Act does not apply to—

(*a*) an arbitration under an agreement providing for the reference to, or the settlement by, arbitration of any question relating to the terms or conditions of employment or the remuneration of any employees, including persons employed by or under the State or local authorities, or

(*b*) an arbitration under section 70 of the Industrial Relations Act, 1946 (No. 26 of 1946).

Operation of Parts II and III

6.—(1) Part II of this Act shall not affect any arbitration under an arbitration agreement which has commenced before the operative date, but shall apply to any arbitration commenced on or before the operative date under an arbitration agreement made before the operative date.

(2) Part III of this Act shall not affect any arbitration under any other Act which has commenced before the operative date, but shall apply to any arbitration commenced on or after the operative date under any other Act passed before, on, or after the operative date.

7.—Any person who, upon any examination upon oath or affirmation before an arbitrator or umpire or in any affidavit in proceedings before an arbitrator or umpire, wilfully and corruptly gives false evidence or wilfully and corruptly swears or affirms anything which is false, being convicted thereof, shall be liable to the penalties for wilful and corrupt perjury.

Penalty for
giving false
evidence

8.—(1) The enactments mentioned in column (2) of the Third Schedule to this Act are (except in relation to arbitrations under arbitration agreements commenced before the operative date) hereby repealed to the extent mentioned in column (3) of that Schedule.

Repeals

(2) Any enactment or instrument referring to any enactment repealed by this Act shall be construed as referring to this Act.

PART II

Arbitration under Arbitration Agreements

9.—The authority of the arbitrator or umpire appointed by or by virtue of an arbitration agreement shall, unless a contrary intention is expressed in the agreement, be irrevocable except by leave of the Court.

Authority
of
arbitrators
and umpires
to be
irrevocable

10.—(1) An arbitration agreement shall not be discharged by the death of any party thereto, either as respects the deceased or any other party, but shall in such an event be enforceable by or against the personal representatives of the deceased.

Death of
party

(2) The authority of an arbitrator shall not be revoked by the death of any party by whom he was appointed.

(3) Nothing in this section shall be taken to affect the operation of any enactment or rule of law by virtue of which any right of action is extinguished by the death of a person.

11.—(1) In this section the word "assignee" means the Official Assignee in Bankruptcy and includes the assignee (if any) chosen by the creditors to act with the Official Assignee in Bankruptcy.

Provisions
in case of
bankruptcy

(2) Where an arbitration agreement forms part of a contract to which a bankrupt is a party, the agreement shall, if the assignee or trustee in bankruptcy does not disclaim the contract, be enforceable by or against him so far as it relates to any difference arising out of, or in connection with, such contract.

(3) Where—

    (*a*) a person who has been adjudged bankrupt had, before the commencement of the bankruptcy, become a party to an arbitration agreement, and

    (*b*) any matter to which the agreement applies requires to be determined in connection with or for the purposes of the bankruptcy proceedings, and

(*c*) the case is one to which subsection (2) of this section does not apply,

then, any other party to the agreement or the assignee or, with the consent of the committee of inspection, the trustee in bankruptcy may apply to the court having jurisdiction in the bankruptcy proceedings for an order directing that the matter in question shall be referred to arbitration in accordance with the agreement and that court may, if it is of opinion that having regard to all the circumstances of the case, the matter ought to be determined by arbitration, make an order accordingly.

12.—[Repealed by s. 4 of the Arbitration Act, 1980].

13.—Where relief by way of interpleader is granted and it appears to the Court that the claims in question are matters to which an arbitration agreement, to which the claimants are parties, applies, the Court may direct the issue between the claimants to be determined in accordance with the agreement.

Reference of interpleader issues to arbitration

Arbitrators and Umpires

14.—Unless a contrary intention is expressed therein, every arbitration agreement shall, if no other mode of reference is provided, be deemed to include a provision that the reference shall be to a single arbitrator.

When reference is to be to a single arbitrator

15.—(1) Where—

(*a*) an arbitration agreement provides that the reference shall be to two arbitrators, one to be appointed by each party, and

(*b*) either of the appointed arbitrators refuses to act, or is incapable of acting, or dies,

Power of parties in certain cases to supply vacancy

then, unless the agreement expresses a contrary intention, the party, who appointed the arbitrator so refusing to act, becoming incapable of acting or dying, may appoint a new arbitrator in his place.

(2) (*a*) Where—

(i) an arbitration agreement provides that the reference shall be to two arbitrators, one to be appointed by each party, and

(ii) on such a reference one party fails to appoint an arbitrator, either originally or by way of substitution under subsection (1) of this section, for seven clear days after the other party, having appointed his arbitrator, has served the party making default with notice to make the appointment.

then unless a contrary intention is expressed in the agreement, the party who has appointed an arbitrator may appoint that arbitrator to act as sole arbitrator in the reference, and his award shall be binding on both parties as if he had been appointed by consent.

(*b*) The Court may set aside any appointment made under paragraph (*a*) of this subsection.

16.—(1) Unless a contrary agreement is expressed therein, every arbitration Umpires agreement shall, where the reference is to two arbitrators, be deemed to include a provision that the two arbitrators shall appoint an umpire immediately after they are themselves appointed.

(2) Unless a contrary intention is expressed therein, every arbitration agreement shall, where such a provision is applicable to the reference, be deemed to include a provision that if the arbitrators have delivered to any party to the arbitration agreement, or to the umpire, a notice in writing stating that they cannot agree, the umpire may forthwith enter upon the reference in lieu of the arbitrators, but nothing in this subsection shall be construed as preventing the umpire from sitting with the arbitrators and hearing the evidence.

(3) At any time after the appointment of an umpire, however appointed, the Court may, on the application of any parts to the reference and notwithstanding anything to the contrary in the arbitration agreement, order that the umpire shall enter upon the reference in lieu of the arbitrators and as if he were a sole arbitrator.

17.—(1) Where an arbitration agreement provides that the reference shall be Agreements to three arbitrators, one to be appointed by each party and the third to be for appointed by the two appointed by the parties, the agreement shall have effect reference to three as if it provided for the appointment of an umpire, and not for the appointment arbitrators of a third arbitrator, by the two arbitrators appointed by the parties.

(2) Where an arbitration agreement provides that the reference shall be to three arbitrators to be appointed otherwise than as is mentioned in subsection (1) of this section, the award of any two of the arbitrators shall be binding.

18.—In any of the following cases— Power of
    (*a*) where— Court in
        (i) an arbitration agreement provides that the reference shall be certain cases to
           to a single arbitrator, and appoint an
        (ii) all the parties do not, after differences have arisen, concur in arbitrator or
           the appointment of an arbitrator; umpire
    (*b*) if—
        (i) an appointed arbitrator refuses to act, or is incapable of acting or dies, and
        (ii) the arbitration agreement does not show that it was intended that the vacancy should not be supplied, and
        (iii) the parties do not suppy the vacancy;
    (*c*) where the parties or two arbitrators are at liberty to appoint an umpire or third arbitrator and do not appoint him;
    (*d*) where two arbitrators are required to appoint an umpire and do not appoint him;

(*e*) where—

> (i) an appointed umpire or third arbitrator refuses to act, or is incapable of acting, or dies, and
>
> (ii) the arbitration agreement does not show that it was intended that the vacancy should not be supplied, and
>
> (iii) the parties or arbitrators do not supply the vacancy,

the following provisions shall have effect—

(1) any party may serve the other parties or the arbitrators, as the case may be, with a written notice to appoint or, as the case may be, concur in appointing an arbitrator, umpire or third arbitrator,

(2) if the appointment is not made within seven clear days after the service of the notice, the Court may, on the application of the party who gave the notice, appoint an arbitrator, umpire or third arbitrator, who shall have the like powers to act in the reference and make an award as if he had been appointed by consent of all parties.

Witnesses, Security for Costs, Discovery of Documents, etc.

Powers of arbitrators and umpires as to witnesses

19.—(1) Unless a contrary intention is expressed therein every arbitration agreement shall, where such a provision is applicable to the reference, be deemed to contain a provision that the parties to the reference, and all persons claiming through them respectively, shall, subject to any legal objection, submit to be examined by the arbitrator or umpire, on oath or affirmation, in relation to the matters in dispute and shall, subject to any legal objection, produce before the arbitrator or umpire all documents (other than documents the production of which could not be compelled on the trial of an action) within their possession or power respectively which may be required or called for, and do all such other things which during the proceedings on the reference the arbitrator or umpire may require.

(2) Unless a contrary intention is expressed therein, every arbitration agreement shall, where such a provision is applicable to the reference, be deemed to contain a provision that the witnesses on the reference shall, if the arbitrator or umpire thinks fit, be examined on oath or affirmation.

(3) An arbitrator or umpire shall, unless a contrary intention is expressed in an arbitration agreement, have power to administer oaths to, or take the affirmation of, the parties to and witnesses on a reference under the agreement.

Powers of parties to a reference to compel attendance of witnesses

20.—Any party to a reference under an arbitration agreement may sue out an order in the nature of a writ of subpoena ad testificandum or of a writ of subpoena duces tecum, but no person shall be compelled under any such order to produce any document which he could not be compelled to produce on the trial of an action.

21.—The Court may order that an order in the nature of a writ of habeas corpus ad testificandum shall issue to bring up a prisoner for examination before an arbitrator or umpire.

Power of
Court to
compel
attendance
of prisoner
as a witness

22.—(1) The Court shall have, for the purpose of and in relation to a reference, the same power of making orders in respect of—

Orders by
Court in
relation to
security for
costs
discovery of
documents
etc.

    (*a*) security for costs;

    (*b*) discovery and inspection of documents and interrogatories;

    (*c*) the giving of evidence by affidavit;

    (*d*) examination on oath of any witness before an officer of the Court or any other person, and the issue of a commission or request for the examination of a witness out of the jurisdiction;

    (*e*) the preservation, interim custody or sale of any goods which are the subject matter of the reference;

    (*f*) securing the amount in dispute in the reference;

    (*g*) the detention, preservation or inspection of any property or thing which is the subject of the reference or as to which any question may arise therein, and authorising for any of the purposes aforesaid any persons to enter upon or into any land or building in the possession of any party to the reference, or authorising any samples to be taken or any observation to be made or experiment to be tried which may be necessary or expedient for the purpose of obtaining full information or evidence; and

    (*h*) interim injunctions or the appointment of a receiver,

as it has for the purpose of and in relation to an action or matter in the Court.

(2) Nothing in subsection (1) of this section shall be taken to prejudice any power which may be vested in an arbitrator or umpire of making orders with respect to any of the matters mentioned in the said subsection.

Provisions as the Awards

23.—(1) Subject to subsection (2) of section 36 of this Act and anything to the contrary in the arbitration agreement, an arbitrator or umpire shall have power to make an award at any time.

Time for
making an
award

(2) The time, if any, limited for making an award, whether under this Act or otherwise, may from time to time be enlarged by order of the Court or by agreement in writing of the parties, whether that time has expired or not.

24.—(1) The Court may, on the application of any party to a reference, remove an arbitrator or umpire who fails to use all reasonable dispatch in entering on and proceeding with the reference and making an award.

Removal of
arbitrator or
umpire on
failure to
use due
dispatch

(2) An arbitrator or umpire who is removed by the Court under subsection (1) of this section shall not be entitled to receive any remuneration in respect of his services.

(3) For the purposes of this section the expression "proceeding with a reference" includes, in a case where two arbitrators are unable to agree, giving notice of that fact to the parties and to the umpire.

Interim
award

25.—Unless a contrary intention is expressed therein, every arbitration agreement shall, where such a provision is applicable to the reference, be deemed to contain a provision that the arbitrator or umpire may, if he thinks fit, make an interim award.

Specific
performance

26.—Unless a contrary intention is expressed therein, every arbitration agreement shall, where such a provision is applicable to the reference, be deemed to contain a provision that the arbitrator or umpire shall have the same power as the Court to order specific performance of any contract other than a contract relating to land or any interest in land.

Awards to
be final

27.—Unless a contrary intention is expressed therein, every arbitration agreement shall, where such a provision is applicable to the reference, be deemed to contain a provision that the award to be made by the arbitrator or umpire shall be final and binding on the parties and the persons claiming under them respectively.

Power to
correct slips

28.—Unless a contrary intention is expressed in the arbitration agreement, the arbitrator or umpire shall have power to correct in an award any clerical mistake or error arising from any accidental slip or omission.

Costs, Fees and Interest

Costs of
reference
and award
to be in the
discretion
of the
arbitrator or
umpire

29.—(1) Unless a contrary intention is expressed therein, every arbitration agreement shall be deemed to include a provision that the costs of the reference and award shall be in the discretion of the arbitrator or umpire who may direct to and by whom and in what manner those costs or any part thereof shall be paid, and may, with the consent of the parties, tax or settle the amount of costs to be so paid or any part thereof, and may award costs to be paid as between solicitor and client.

(2) Where an award directs any costs to be paid, then, unless the arbitrator or umpire, with the consent of the parties, taxes or settles the amount thereof—

> (*a*) the costs shall be taxed and ascertained by a Taxing Master,
> (*b*) the procedure to obtain taxation and the rules, regulations and scales of costs of the Court relative to taxation and to the review thereof shall apply to the costs to be so taxed and ascertained as if the award were a judgment or order of the Court.

Avoidance
of certain
provisions
as to costs
in
arbitration
agreements

30.—(1) Any provision in an arbitration agreement to the effect that the parties or any party thereto shall in any event pay their or his own costs of the reference or award or any part thereof shall be void, and this Part shall, in the case of an arbitration agreement containing any such provision, have effect as if that provision were not contained therein.

(2) Nothing in subsection (1) of this section shall invalidate any such provision as is mentioned in that subsection when it is part of an agreement to submit to arbitration a dispute which has arisen before the making of that agreement.

31.—If no provision is made by an award with respect to the costs of the reference, any party to the reference may, within fourteen days of the publication of the award or such further time as the Court may direct, apply to the arbitrator or umpire for an order directing by and to whom those costs shall be paid, and thereupon the arbitrator or umpire shall, after hearing any party who may desire to be heard, amend his award by adding thereto such directions as he may think proper with respect to the payment of the costs of the reference. *Application to arbitrator or umpire to give directions as to costs where award contains no provisions*

32.—Section 3 of the Legal Practitioners (Ireland) Act, 1876, (which empowers a court before which any proceeding has been heard or is pending to charge property recovered or preserved in the proceeding with the payment of solicitors' costs) shall apply as if an arbitration were a proceeding in the Court, and the Court may make declarations and orders accordingly. *Application of section 3 of Legal Practitioners (Ireland) Act, 1876, to solicitors' costs in arbitrations*

33.—(1) If in any case an arbitrator or umpire refuses to deliver his award except on payment of the fees demanded by him the Court may, on an application for the purpose, order that the arbitrator or umpire shall deliver the award to the applicant on payment into Court by the applicant of the fees demanded, and further that the fees demanded shall be taxed by a Taxing Master and that out of the money paid into Court there shall be paid out to the arbitrator or umpire by way of fees such sum as may be found reasonable on taxation and that the balance of the money, if any, shall be paid out to the applicant. *Taxation of arbitrator's or umpire's fee*

(2) Any application for the purpose of this section may be made by any party to the reference unless the fees demanded have been fixed by a written agreement between him and the arbitrator or umpire.

(3) A taxation of fees under this section may be reviewed in the same manner as a taxation of costs.

(4) The arbitrator or umpire shall be entitled to appear and be heard on any taxation or review of taxation under this section.

34.—A sum directed to be paid by an award shall, unless the award otherwise directs, carry interest as from the date of the award and at the same rate as a judgment debt. *Interest on awards*

Special Cases, Remission and Setting aside of Awards, Removal of
Arbitrator or Umpire, and Relief where Arbitrator not impartial or
Questions of Fraud involved

Statement
of case by
arbitrator or
umpire

35.—(1) An arbitrator or umpire may, and shall if so directed by the Court, state—

>   (*a*) any question of law arising in the course of the reference, or
>   (*b*) any award or any part of the award,

in the form of a special case for the decision of the Court.

(2) A special case with respect to an interim award or with respect to a question of law arising in the course of a reference may be stated, or may be ordered by the Court to be stated, notwithstanding that proceedings under the reference are still pending.

Power of
Court to
remit award

36.—(1) In all cases of reference to arbitration, the Court may from time to time remit the matters referred or any of them to the reconsideration of the arbitrator or umpire.

Power of
Court to
remove
arbitrator or
umpire on
ground of
misconduct

(2) Where an award is remitted, the arbitrator or umpire shall, unless the order otherwise directs, make his award within three months after the date of the order.

37.—Where an arbitrator or umpire has misconducted himself or the proceedings, the Court may remove him.

Power of
Court to set
aside award
on ground
of
misconduct

38.—(1) Where—

>   (*a*) an arbitrator or umpire has misconducted himself or the proceed-
>   ings, or
>   (*b*) an arbitration or award has been improperly procured,

the Court may set the award aside.

(2) Where an application is made to set aside an award, the Court may order that any moneys payable by the award shall be brought into Court or otherwise secured pending the determination of the application.

Power of
Court to
give relief
where
arbitrator is
not
impartial or
dispute
referred
involves
question of
fraud

39.—(1) Where—

>   (*a*) an agreement between any parties provides that disputes which may
>   arise in the future between them shall be referred to an arbitrator
>   named or designated in the agreement, and
>   (*b*) after a dispute has arisen any party, on the ground that the arbitrator
>   so named or designated is not or may not be impartial, applies to
>   the Court for leave to revoke the authority of the arbitrator or for
>   an injunction to restrain any other party or the arbitrator from
>   proceeding with the arbitration,

it shall not be a ground for refusing the application that the said party at the time when he made the agreement knew, or ought to have known, that the arbitrator, by reason of his relation towards any other party to the agreement or of his connection with the subject referred, might not be impartial.

(2) Where—

(*a*) an agreement between any parties provides that disputes which may arise in the future between them shall be referred to arbitration, and

(*b*) a dispute which so arises involves the question whether any party has been guilty of fraud,

the Court shall, so far as may be necessary to enable the question to be determined by the Court, have power to order that the agreement shall cease to have effect and power to give leave to revoke the authority of any arbitrator or umpire appointed by or by virtue of the agreement.

(3) In any case where by virtue of this section the Court has power to order that any arbitration agreement shall cease to have effect or to give leave to revoke the authority of any arbitrator or umpire, the Court may refuse to stay any action brought in breach of the agreement.

40.—(1) Where an arbitrator (not being a sole arbitrator) or two or more arbitrators (not being all the arbitrators) or an umpire who has not entered on the reference is or are removed by the Court, the Court may, on the application of any party to the arbitration agreement, appoint a person or persons to act as arbitrator or arbitrators or umpire in place of the person or persons so removed.

Power of Court where arbitrator is removed or authority of arbitrator is revoked

(2) Where—

(*a*) the authority of the arbitrator or arbitrators or umpire is revoked by leave of the Court, or

(*b*) a sole arbitrator or all the arbitrators or an umpire who has entered on the reference is or are removed by the Court,

the Court may, on the application of any party to the arbitration agreement, either—

(i) appoint a person to act as sole arbitrator in place of the person of persons removed, or

(ii) order that the arbitration agreement shall cease to have effect with respect to the dispute referred.

(3) A person appointed under this section by the Court as an arbitrator or umpire shall have the like power to act in the reference and to make an award if he had been appointed in accordance with the terms of the arbitration agreement.

(4) Where it is provided (whether by means of a provision in an arbitration agreement or otherwise) that an award under an arbitration agreement shall be a condition precedent to the bringing of an action with respect to any matter to which the agreement applies, the Court, if it orders (whether under this section or any other enactments) that the agreement shall cease to have effect as regards any particular dispute, may further order that the provision making an award a condition precedent to the bringing of an action shall also cease to have effect as regards that dispute.

Enforcement of Award

Enforcement of award

41.—An award on an arbitration agreement may, by leave of the Court, be enforced in the same manner as a judgment or order to the same effect and, where leave is so given, judgment may be entered in terms of the award.

Application of statutes of limitation to arbitration under arbitration agreements

Limitation of Time for Commencing Arbitration Proceedings

42.—The statutes of limitation shall apply to an arbitration under an arbitration agreement as they apply to actions in the Court.

Accrual for purposes of statutes of limitation of right of action

43.—Notwithstanding any term in an arbitration agreement to the effect that no cause of action shall accrue in respect of any matter required by the agreement to be referred until an award is made under the agreement, a cause of action shall, for the purpose of the statutes of limitation (whether in their application to arbitrations or to other proceedings), be deemed to have accrued in respect of any such matter at the time when it would have accrued but for that term in the agreement.

Power of Court to extend period of limitation where it sets aside award or orders arbitration to cease to have effect

44.—Where the Court orders that an award be set aside or orders, after the commencement of an arbitration, that the arbitration should cease to have effect with respect to the dispute referred, the Court may further order that the period between the commencement of the arbitration and the date of the order of the Court shall be excluded in computing the time prescribed by the statutes of limitation for the commencement of the proceedings (including arbitration) with respect to the dispute referred.

Power of Court to extend time for commencing arbitration proceedings, where agreement provides that claims are to be barred unless proceedings are commenced within a specified time

45.—Where—

(*a*) the terms of an agreement to refer future disputes to arbitration provide that any claims to which the agreement applies may be barred unless notice to appoint an arbitrator is given or an arbitrator is appointed or some other step to commence arbitration proceedings is taken within a time fixed by the agreement, and

(*b*) a dispute arises to which the agreement applies,

the Court, if it is of opinion that in the circumstances of the case undue hardship would otherwise be caused, and notwithstanding that the time so fixed has expired, may on such terms, if any, as the justice of the case may require, but without prejudice to section 42 of this Act, extend the time for such period as it thinks proper.

Extension of section 496 of the Merchant Shipping Act, 1894

46.—In subsection (3) of section 496 of the Merchant Shipping Act, 1894 (which requires a sum deposited with a wharfinger by an owner of goods to be repaid unless legal proceedings are instituted by the shipowner) the references to legal proceedings shall be construed as including references to arbitration.

Terms of Orders

47.—(1) Any order made under this Part by a court may be made on such terms as to costs or otherwise as that court thinks just. Terms of orders

(2) Subsection (1) of this section shall not apply to an order made under subsection (2) of section 12 of this Act.

PART III

ARBITRATION UNDER OTHER ACTS

48.—(1) In this section, the expression "the excluded provisions" means the following provisions of this Act, subsection (1) of section 10, section 11, subsection (2) of section 12, and sections 13, 30, 39, 40, 45, and 46. Application of Parts I and II to arbitrations under other Acts

(2) Parts I and II of this Act (except the excluded provisions) shall apply to every arbitration under any other Act as if the arbitration were pursuant to an arbitration agreement and as if that other Act were an arbitration agreement, except in so far as Part II of this Act is inconsistent with that other Act or with any rules or procedure authorised or recognised thereby.

PART IV

REFERENCES UNDER ORDERS OF THE COURT

49.—(1) If, in any cause or matter (including any cause or matter to which a State authority is a party, but excluding a criminal proceeding at the suit of the Attorney General), the question in dispute consists wholly or in part of matters of account, the Court or the Circuit Court may at any time order the whole cause or matter or any question or issue of fact arising therein to be tried before an arbitrator agreed on by the parties or before an officer of the Court or the Circuit Court (as the case may be), upon such terms as to costs or otherwise as the Court or Circuit Court (as the case may be) thinks just. Power of Court and Circuit Court to refer in certain cases

(2) The references in sections 50 and 52 of this Act and the first and second references in section 51 of this Act to the Court shall be construed as including references to the Circuit Court.

50.—(1) In all cases of references to an arbitrator under an order of the Court under section 49 of this Act, the arbitrator shall be deemed to be an officer of the Court, and, subject to rules of court, shall have such authority and conduct the reference in such manner as the Court may direct. Power of arbitrators in references under section 49

(2) The award of an arbitrator on any reference under section 49 of this Act shall, unless set aside by the Court, be equivalent to the verdict of a jury.

(3) The remuneration to be paid to an arbitrator to whom any matter is referred under section 49 of this Act shall be determined by the Court.

Court to
have powers
as in
references
under
arbitration
agreements

51.—The Court shall, in relation to references under an order of the Court made under section 49 of the Act, have all the powers which are by Part II of this Act conferred on the Court in relation to references under arbitration agreements.

Statement of
case
pending
arbitration

52.—An arbitrator on any reference under section 49 of this Act may at any stage of the proceedings under the reference, and shall, if so directed by the Court, state in the form of a special case for the opinion of the Court any question of law arising in the course of the reference.

Powers of
Supreme
Court

53.—The Supreme Court shall have all such powers as are conferred by this Part on the Court.

THIRD SCHEDULE

ENACTMENTS REPEALED

Session and Chapter. (1)	Title or Short Title. (2)	Extent of Repeal. (3)
10 Will 3, c. 14 (Ir.)	An Act for determining differences by arbitration.	The whole Act.
3 & 4 Vic. c. 105.	The Debtors (Ireland) Act, 1840.	Sections 63 and 64.
19 & 20 Vic. c. 102.	The Common Law Procedure Amendment Act (Ireland), 1856.	Sections 6 to 20.
40 & 41 Vic. c. 57.	The Supreme Court of Judicature Act (Ireland), 1877.	In section 60, the words "the provisions contained in the sections of 'the Common Law Procedure Act (Ireland), 1856,' in reference to arbitration shall apply to the High Court of Justice and the several Divisions thereof, and the Judges of the same respectively, in the same manner as formerly to the Superior Courts of Common Law and the Judges of the same respectively."

Statute of Limitations, 1957

Number 6 of 1957

AN ACT TO CONSOLIDATE WITH AMENDMENTS CERTAIN ENACT-
MENTS RELATING TO THE LIMITATION OF ACTIONS AND
ARBITRATIONS. [*2nd May* 1957]

BE IT ENACTED BY THE OIREACHTAS AS FOLLOWS:—

PART IV

APPLICATION OF THIS ACT AND OTHER LIMITATION ENACTMENTS TO ARBITRATIONS

73.—In this Part of this Act— Interpretation (Part IV)
"the Court" means the High Court.

74.—(1) For the purposes of this Act and of any other limitation enactment, Commencement of arbitration an arbitration shall be deemed to be commenced when one party to the arbitration agreement serves on the other party or parties a written notice requiring him or them to appoint or concur in appointing an arbitrator or, where the arbitration agreement provides that the reference shall be to a person named or designated in the agreement, requiring him or them to submit the dispute to the person so named or designated.

(2)   (*a*) A notice under subsection (1) of this section may be served—

    (i) by delivering it to the person on whom it is to be served,

    (ii) by leaving it at the place in the State at which that person ordinarily resides or carries on business,

    (iii) by sending it by registered post in an envelope addressed to that person at the place in the State at which he ordinarily resides or carries on business,

    (iv) in any other manner provided for in the arbitration agreement.

  (*b*) For the purposes of this subsection, a company registered under the Companies Acts, 1908 to 1924, shall be deemed to carry on business at its registered office in the State and every other body corporate and every unincorporated body shall be deemed to carry on business at its principal office or place of business in the State. Application of Act and other limitation enactments to arbitrations

75.—This Act and any other limitation enactment shall apply to arbitrations as they apply to actions in the Court.

143

76.—Notwithstanding any term in an arbitration agreement to the effect that no cause of action shall accrue in respect of any matter required by the agreement to be referred until an award is made under the agreement, the cause of action shall, for the purpose of this Act and of any other limitation enactment (whether in their application to arbitrations or to other proceedings), be deemed to have accrued in respect of any such matter at the time when it would have accrued but for that term in the agreement.

Accrual of cause of action where agreement makes award thereunder a condition precedent to commencement of action

77.—Where the Court orders that an award be set aside or orders, after the commencement of an arbitration, that the arbitration shall cease to have effect with respect to the dispute referred, the Court may further order that the period between the commencement of the arbitration and the date of the order of the Court shall be excluded in computing the time fixed by this Act or any other limitation enactment for the commencement of proceedings (including arbitration) with respect to the dispute referred.

Power of Court to extend time where it sets aside award or orders arbitration to cease to have effect

78.—This Part of this Act shall apply to an arbitration under an Act as well as to an arbitration pursuant to an arbitration agreement, and section 74 of this Act shall have effect, in relation to an arbitration under an Act, as if, for the references to the arbitration agreement, there were substituted references to such of the provisions of the Act or of any order, scheme, rules, regulations or bye-laws made thereunder as relate to the arbitration.

Application of Part IV to abritrations under other Acts

79.—This Act shall not apply to—
>   (*a*) any arbitration for which a period of limitation is fixed by any other enactment, or
>   (*b*) any arbitration to which a State authority is a party and for which, if that State authority were a private individual, a period of limitation would be fixed by any other enactment.

Saving for other enactments relating to limitation of arbitrations

80.—Nothing in this Act shall effect an arbitration commenced before the operative date or the title to any property which is the subject of any such arbitration.

Arbitrations pending on the operative date

Arbitration Act, 1980

Number 7 of 1980

AN ACT TO ENABLE EFFECT TO BE GIVEN TO THE CONVENTION ON THE RECOGNITION AND ENFORCEMENT OF FOREIGN AR-BITRAL AWARDS DONE AT NEW YORK ON THE 10th DAY OF JUNE, 1958, AND TO CERTAIN PROVISIONS OF THE CONVEN-TION ON THE SETTLEMENT OF INVESTMENT DISPUTES BE-TWEEN STATES AND NATIONALS OF OTHER STATES OPENED FOR SIGNATURES IN WASHINGTON ON THE 18th DAY OF MARCH, 1965, AND OTHERWISE TO AMEND THE ARBITRA-TION ACT, 1954. [*4th June*, 1980]

· BE IT ENACTED BY THE OIREACHTAS AS FOLLOWS:

PART I

PRELIMINARY AND GENERAL

1.—(1) This Act may be cited as the Arbitration Act, 1980.

(2) The Arbitration Act, 1954, and this Act may be cited together as the Arbitration Acts, 1954 and 1980.

Short title and collective citation

2.—In this Act—

"arbitration agreement" means an agreement in writing (including an agreement contained in an exchange of letters or telegrams) to submit to arbitration present or future differences capable of settlement by arbitration;

"the Principal Act" means the Arbitration Act, 1954.

Definitions

3.—*Parts III* and *IV* of this Act shall come into operation on such day or days as the Minister for Justice may by order appoint.

Commencement

4.—Section 12 of the Principal Act is hereby repealed.

Repeal

PART II

EFFECT OF ARBITRATION AGREEMENTON COURT PROCEEDINGS

5.—(1) If any party to an arbitration agreement, or any person claiming through or under him, commences any proceedings in any court against any other party to such agreement, or any person claiming through or under him, in

Staying court proceedings where party proves arbitration agreement respect of any matter agreed to be referred to arbitration, any party to the proceedings may at any time after an appearance has been entered, and before delivering any pleadings or takings any other steps in the proceedings, apply to the court to stay the proceedings, and the court, unless it is satisfied that the arbitration agreement is null and void, inoperative or incapable of being performed or that there is not in fact any dispute between the parties with regard to the matter agreed to be referred, shall make an order staying the proceedings.

(2) Nothing in this section shall be constued as limiting or otherwise affecting the power conferred on the High Court pursuant to section 39(3) of the Principal Act to refuse to stay any action brought in breach of an arbitration agreement.

PART III (ss. 6-11)

PART IV (ss. 12-17)

Rules of the Superior Courts

SI No. 15 of 1986

ORDER 56

ARBITRATION

1. In this Order:

"the Acts" means the Arbitration Acts, 1954 and 1980;

"party" includes the personal representative of a deceased party; words and phrases defined in the Acts have the same meanings.

2. An application to stay proceedings in pursuance of section 5 of the Arbitration Act, 1980, may be made by motion in such proceedings on notice to the plaintiff.

3. Where relief may by way of interpleader is granted, an application to direct the issue between the claimants to be determined by arbitration in pursuance of section 13 of the Arbitration Act, 1954, may be made by any party at the hearing of the application or proceedings in which such relief is granted or at the conclusion of such hearing.

4. An application by any party to a reference under an arbitration agreement—

      (*a*) to appoint an arbitrator or umpire, or

      (*b*) to remove an arbitrator or umpire, with or without an application to appoint another person in his place, or

      (*c*) to remit an award to an arbitrator or umpire, or

      (*d*) to direct an arbitrator or umpire to state a special case for the Court, or

      (*e*) to set aside an award, or

      (*f*) to enforce an award in pursuance of section 41 of the Arbitration Act, 1954,

may be made by special summons, to which the other party to the reference, and (in the case of an application under paragraph (*b*) or paragraph (*d*)) the arbitrator or umpire, shall be defendants. An application to remit or set aside an award shall be made within six weeks after the award has been made and published to the parties, or within such further time as may be allowed by the Court.

5. An application to enlarge the time for making an award under an arbitration agreement may be made by any party to the reference by motion on notice to the other party and to the arbitrator or umpire (as the case may be) or may be made by the arbitrator or umpire by motion on notice to the parties to the reference.

6. An application for the delivery of an award and taxation of the fees of an arbitrator or umpire in pursuance of section 33 of the Arbitration Act, 1954, may be made by any party to the reference by motion on notice to the arbitrator or umpire.

7. Any application to the Court under or in pursuance of the Act, for which provision is not made by rules 2 to 6, may be made by a party to a reference under an arbitration agreement by motion on notice to the other party.

8. Every originating notice of motion under this Order (other than an application under section 11(3) of the Arbitration Act, 1954), shall be entitled in the matter of the arbitration to which it relates and in the matter of the Act, and the provisions of Order 5 rule 7 shall apply *mutatis mutandis* to such notices of motion.

Arbitration Rules of the Chartered Institute of Arbitrators (Irish Branch)

(Adopted to take effect from 1 April 1990)

RULE 1 — APPLICABILITY

1.1 Where any agreement, submission or reference provides for arbitration under the Arbitration Rules of The Charterd Institute of Arbitrators — Irish Branch ('the Branch') the arbitration shall be conducted in accordance with the following Rules or such amended Rules as the Branch may adopt from time to time and which shall have taken effect before the commencement of the arbitration.

1.2 In any other circumstances where a dispute is referred to arbitration these Rules may be used in whole or in part by agreement of the parties.

RULE 2 — SINGULAR & PLURAL

In the following Rules words importing the singular also include the plural and vice versa where the context requires and in particular the expression 'Arbitrator' includes all the Arbitrators where more than one has been appointed.

RULE 3 — REQUEST FOR NOMINATION OF ARBITRATOR

Where a request for the nomination of an arbitrator is made to the Branch, the Request for Nomination of Arbitrator form should be completed and sent to the Branch at 5 Wilton Place, Dublin 2.

RULE 4 — SELECTION OF ARBITRATOR

On accepting a Request for Nomination of Arbitrator the Branch (unless all the parties have previously agreed on an Arbitrator) shall select and nominate an Arbitrator to determine the dispute and shall advise the parties who shall formally appoint the Arbitrator.

RULE 5 — NUMBER OF ARBITRATORS

5.1 Unless the parties have agreed otherwise the nomination shall be of a single Arbitrator, usually but not necessarily chosen from the Branch's own Panels of Arbitrators. In making a nomination the Branch shall take into consideration any agreement reached or representation made by the parties.

5.2 If the parties have each nominated an Arbitrator the Branch shall nominate those Arbitrators together with a sufficient number of additional Arbitrators, selected by the Branch, to ensure the total numbers of Arbitrators is uneven.

RULE 6 — CHAIRMAN OF TRIBUNAL

The Branch shall nominate the Arbitrator or one of the Arbitrators it selects as the Chairman of the arbitral tribunal.

RULE 7 — REPLACEMENT OF ARBITRATOR

If after appointment any Arbitrator dies, refuses, fails or in the opinion of the Branch becomes unable or unfit to act, the Branch shall upon request appoint another Arbitrator in his place.

RULE 8 — SUITABILITY OF ARBITRATOR

In selecting an Arbitrator the Branch shall so far as possible have regard to the nature of the contract and to the nature and circumstances of the dispute.

RULE 9 — INDEPENDENCE AND IMPARTIALITY OF ARBITRATORS

Any Arbitrator (whether or not nominated by the parties) conducting an arbitration under these Rules shall be and shall remain at all times wholly independent and impartial and shall not act as advocate for any party.

RULE 10 — EXTENSION OF PROCEEDINGS

Nothing in these Rules shall preclude an Arbitrator from acting, where all the parties involved so agree, in Representative Proceedings, Third Party Proceedings or Consolidated Proceedings.

RULE 11 — COMMUNICATIONS

11.1 Where a party sends any communication (including any notice or Statement made under these Rules) to the Arbitrator, it shall include a copy for the Arbitrator and also send copies to all the other parties at the same time and confirm to the Arbitrator that it has done so.

11.2 The Arbitrator shall likewise copy any communication to a party to all the other parties at the same time.

RULE 12 — ADDRESS OF PARTY

For the purpose of all communications during the proceedings the address of a party shall be that set out in the Request for Nomination of Arbitrator or such other addresses as the parties shall later agree or as any party shall notify to the Arbitrator or if there be no such address its last known place of business or its last known address.

RULE 13 — DELIVERY OF COMMUNICATION

13.1 Any notice or communication in any arbitration under these Rules shall be deemed to have been properly delivered if dispatched by post, cable, telex, facsimile transmission or by hand to the address notified to the Arbitrator by the party concerned as the address for service or as provided in Rule 12.

13.2 If any party to whom a notice or communication has to be sent for the purpose of these Rules cannot be found or if for any reason service upon such party cannot readily be effected in accordance with these Rules, the Arbitrator may dispense with such service upon such party or may order substituted service in such form as the Arbitrator thinks fit.

RULE 14 — JURISDICTION

The Arbitrator shall have the jurisdiction and the powers to direct the procedure in the arbitration necessary to ensure the just expeditious economical and final determination of the dispute as set out in the Schedule of Jurisdiction and Powers of the Arbitrator.

RULE 15 — PROCEDURE

In the absence of any other Directions the procedure of the arbitration shall be that set out in the following Rules.

RULE 16 — DIRECTIONS

Directions from the Arbitrator to the parties shall be in writing or, if given orally, shall be confirmed in writing by the Arbitrator within seven days. With or without preliminary meetings, the Arbitrator shall give Directions for the progress of the arbitration.

RULE 17 — ORDERS

If the parties shall themselves agree upon any interlocutory matters, they shall seek the approval of the Arbitrator thereto and the Arbitrator if he so approves shall incorporate any such agreement in an Order.

RULE 18 — OBJECTIONS

Any application to the Arbitrator on any matter relating to the arbitration shall be in writing. On receiving a copy of such application any party may within seven days thereof make an objection in writing to the Arbitrator and shall send a copy to the applicant and shall notify the Arbitrator that such a copy has been sent. Upon receipt of any such application or objection the Arbitrator may give such Directions as appear to him appropriate with or without hearing the parties.

RULE 19 — ADJOURNMENTS

The Arbitrator may adjourn a meeting or hearing for such period as he may deem appropriate if a party appears by a legal or professional representative without proper notice having been given to the other parties or for such other reason as he may deem sufficient.

RULE 20 — JOINT STATEMENT OF MATTERS IN DISPUTE

Wherever possible, the parties shall prepare a joint statement setting out concisely the matters which are in dispute between them and amounts and other reliefs sought and shall submit that statement to the Arbitrator.

RULE 21 — STATEMENT OF CLAIM, DEFENCE & REPLY

21.1 Unless the Arbitrator directs otherwise, where a joint statement of the matters in dispute cannot be prepared the following procedure shall apply.

21.2 The party who requested the arbitration (*'the Claimant'*) shall send to the Arbitrator a Statement of Claim setting out in sufficient detail the facts and contentions of law on which it relies and the relief it claims.

21.3 The other party (*'the Respondent'*) shall send to the Arbitrator a Statement of Defence stating in sufficient detail which of the facts and contentions of law in the Statement of Claim it admits or denies on what grounds and on what other facts and contentions of law it relies. If it has a counterclaim, this shall be set out in the Statement of Defence as a Statement of Claim.

21.4 After receipt of the Statement of Defence, the Claimant may send the Arbitrator a Statement of Reply.

21.5 Where there is a counterclaim, the Claimant shall send the Arbitrator a Statement of Defence to the counterclaim to which the Respondent may make a Statement of Reply.

21.6 All Statements of Claim, Defence and Reply shall be accompanied by copies (or, if they are especially voluminous, lists) of the essential documents on which the party concerned relies and which have not previously been submitted by any party and, where practicable, by relevant samples.

21.7 After the submission of all the Statements, the Arbitrator shall give Directions for the further conduct of the arbitration.

21.8 The Arbitrator shall determine the time limits within which the Statements of Claim, Defence and Reply are to be submitted.

21.9 At the conclusion of pleadings, the Arbitrator may direct the parties to set out concisely the matters which are then in dispute and may direct the parties to draw up a Scott Schedule.

RULE 22 — MEETINGS & HEARINGS

22.1 The Arbitrator may at any time fix the date, time and place of meetings and hearings in the arbitration and shall give all the parties adequate notice of these. Subject to any adjournment which the Arbitrator may allow, the final hearing shall be continued on successive working days until it is concluded.

22.2 Unless the parties shall agree otherwise the Arbitrator may be accompanied by one pupil grade member of the Institute at meetings or hearings.

22.3 Provided that it gives the Arbitrator and the other parties not less than ten days prior notice, or such shorter notice as may be directed by the Arbitrator, any party may be represented at any meeting or hearing by a legal or other professional practitioner. The appearance of the representative as an advocate shall not prevent his appearance as a witness in the same proceedings provided that the capacity in which he is appearing at any one time is made clear.

22.4 The Arbitrator may in his discretion disallow as costs of the arbitration the fees and expenses of legal representatives of the parties provided that he gives notice of his intention to do so.

RULE 23 — THE AWARD

The Arbitrator shall make his Award in writing and as soon as practicable after the conclusion of the final hearing he shall publish his Award and notify the parties that the Award is ready to be taken up.

RULE 24 — MAJORITY DECISION

Where there is more than one Arbitrator and they disagree on any matter or question they shall decide by a majority; failing a majority, the Chairman alone shall decide.

RULE 25 — SETTLEMENTS

25.1 If before the publication of the Arbitrator's final Award the parties arrive at a settlement of their disputes they shall immediately so notify the Arbitrator in writing.

25.2 The Arbitrator may direct that documents be prepared and signed by all the parties recording the terms of the agreement which unless the parties have otherwise agreed shall be incorporated in an Award.

25.3 If the parties' agreement does not determine all matters in dispute, the outstanding differences shall be settled by the Arbitrator in a further Award or Awards.

RULE 26 — COSTS OF THE ARBITRATOR

26.1 The Arbitrator in his terms of acceptance shall state the basis on which his costs will be charged in accordance with the Schedule of Costs contained herein.

26.2 From the commencement of the arbitration all the parties shall be jointly and severally liable to the Arbitrator for his costs until they are paid.

26.3 The Arbitrator shall specify the total amount of his costs in his Award. Unless all the parties agree otherwise he shall determine (in the exercise of his absolute discretion) which party or parties shall pay his costs.

26.4 After notification by the Arbitrator any party may take up the Award upon payment to the Arbitrator of all his costs then still outstanding whereupon the Arbitrator shall send a copy of the Award to the other party or parties.

26.5 If the Award has not been taken up within ten days of the notification the Arbitrator may by action at law proceed to recover all his outstanding costs from any or all of the parties.

26.6 If the Arbitrator has determined that all or any part of his costs shall be paid by any party other than the party which has already paid them in taking up the Award that party shall have the right to recover the appropriate amount from the party liable for the payment.

26.7 If the arbitration is abandoned, suspended or concluded by agreement or otherwise before the final Award is made the parties shall pay to the Arbitrator his costs incurred to that time in such proportions as they shall agree or failing agreement as the Arbitrator shall determine.

RULE 27 — SIMPLIFIED PROCEDURE

27.1 Where the value of all matters in dispute between the parties does not exceed such sum as may from time to time be determined by the Branch or in any other arbitration where the parties so agree:

27.2 The Branch will nominate a single Arbitrator;

27.3 The Arbitrator may determine the dispute at an informal hearing attended by all the parties;

27.4 Alternatively, the Arbitrator may determine the dispute on the documents submitted to him by the parties, voluntarily or on his Direction, without any hearing.

RULE 28 — EXCLUSION OF LIABILITY

28.1 The Arbitrator and the Branch shall not be liable to any party for any act or omission or negligence in connection with any arbitration conducted under these Rules, save for the consequences of conscious and deliberate wrongdoing.

28.2 After the Award has been made and any corrections and additional Awards made, the Arbitrator and the Branch shall not be under any obligation to make any statement to any person about any matter concerning the arbitration and no party shall seek to make any Arbitrator or the Branch a witness in any legal proceedings arising out of the arbitration and the parties agree that the Arbitrator is not compellable as a witness.

INDEX